Citizenship

Learning to Live as Responsible Citizens

by
Debbie Pincus and Richard J. Ward

illustrated by Elizabeth Powell

Cover by Janet Skiles

Copyright © Good Apple, 1991

ISBN No. 0-86653-608-6

Printing No. 98765432

Good Apple
1204 Buchanan St., Box 299
Carthage, IL 62321-0299

SIMON & SCHUSTER *A Paramount Communications Company*

Dedication

Dedicated to the memories of Dr. William Pincus and Eleanor A. Ward, who in their lives demonstrated strong commitments to their communities.

We also wish to remember Vincent Chin, Yusuf Hawkins, and all those who have suffered at the hands of those people who shirk the responsibilities of citizenship. We acknowledge and commend those citizens who stand against the forces of bigotry and who work for social justice and social change.

GA1327

About the Authors

Debbie Pincus is the Director of Counseling at the College of Mount Saint Vincent and a psychotherapist in private practice in New York City. She has designed and implemented the Interpersonal Communications Program for use in many public and private schools. Ms. Pincus leads workshops and seminars on effective communication, which have received national recognition. She has been selected for inclusion in *Who's Who Among Human Service Professionals* and *Who's Who Among American Women*.

She is author of the books *Sharing, Interactions*, and *Feeling Good About Yourself*, published by Good Apple.

Richard J. Ward is a bullion banker, based in New York City. He has published many articles about a wide range of topics. They include public and private management, gold mine finance, public policy towards natural resources, and the impacts of foreign investments on local peoples in the Third World.

Mr. Ward is active in numerous community and civic organizations which address a variety of concerns about public safety, the welfare of handicapped and disadvantaged children, and wildlife and environmental preservation. He has lived and worked in many parts of the world, including Australia, Venezuela, Colombia, Israel, and Papua New Guinea. Mr. Ward holds master's degrees from Pennsylvania State University and Yale University.

GA1327

Table of Contents

GA1327

GA1327

Foreword

We need more books on citizenship like this one. More importantly, we need more citizens. Too many people consider themselves citizens because they have rights. Their rights, however, are secured only if they participate in a public life where they are responsible for others—not just themselves. There are fewer such citizens these days than we care to acknowledge.

A useful way to think about citizenship is for each of us to ask what our litter philosophy is. Each person has one. Do you litter? If so, where and why? If you don't litter, why? Do you pick up other people's litter? If so, when do you pick it up and for how long? These questions assume there are public spaces, conditions, problems that we share. What we do about them depends on how we are raised and how we are educated. Our assumptions and habits need to be examined and the Pincus/Ward book does just that. Young people need to reflect on what their habits of mind and action are and in so doing find reasons that support or alter them. They need to think about what, in fact, is their unstated litter philosophy.

The questions and exercises in this book also promote conversation. The examination of one's own litter philosophy leads on to the discussion of other points of view. Students learn that there are differences among them. Public spaces, conditions and problems do not yield one answer. They learn that citizenship is not a solitary business but a shared enterprise and often contentious.

If we are to have more citizens, we need to encourage more reflection and conversation. The classroom has to make room for civic literacy as well as other kinds of literacy. Every student should be able to articulate and defend his or her litter philosophy and ask others to do the same. I am pleased that this book challenges those who will read and use it to become thoughtful participants in American public life.

David W. Brown
President
Blackburn College
Carlinville, Illinois
September 28, 1990

GA1327

Introduction

Citizenship, as the term is used in the book, addresses individual responsibilities in three realms: obedience to law, the exercise of free choice, and the realm of social responsibility which lies between. This middle realm is the focus of the book.

Chapter 1 builds awareness as it suggests that the responsibilities of citizenship stem from the students' memberships in various communities. It also addresses concepts such as civil disobedience and the individual's role in the process of social change. Chapters 2, 3, and 4 help students to examine their inherited attitudes and values, to choose among alternative behaviors, and to build skills in addressing community issues.

Chapter 5 presents opportunities for the students to examine the citizenship qualities of a wide range of people. The students must determine what concerns they feel are important as they gain a sense for the dynamic interplay of peoples' individual needs in the community.

Our hope is that students who complete the book will develop a strong commitment to life-long involvement in their communities and will actively pursue agendas which lead to a stronger social fabric. The book tries to elicit discussion and growth as the students are called upon to discover their own views and to examine them from various perspectives. We have attempted to avoid "telling" people what constitutes good or responsible citizenship. We trust that the teacher-led discussions will elicit the growth of responsible activist values.

For the Teacher

The activities in *Citizenship* can be used for students in the 5th, 6th, 7th, 8th, and 9th grades and above. The activities can be approached in a relatively simple or complex fashion and can be easily modified for use at various grade levels. The teacher must select and/or modify the exercise according to grade level and ability.

Activities are designed for group discussions led by the teacher. The learning value of the activities is enhanced if the teacher attempts to draw out students' attitudes and values through debate, role play, and discussion.

Students will derive the greatest value from the exercises in each chapter if the vocabulary exercises at the beginning are first completed. Some chapter exercises direct the students to the glossary, which presents definitions for those terms. In addition, students should make ample use of their own dictionaries to gain the most understanding from the exercises.

It will also facilitate learning to introduce the main concepts found in the chapter at the outset.

GA1327

Quotations are presented throughout the book. They are included to give greater meaning to the work students do and to serve as grist for discussion. The quotations speak wryly and wisely. They reinforce concepts and draw attention to the difficulty individuals face in being responsible citizens.

The quotations are meant to be discussed. Students should be encouraged to voice their opinions about the quotes' meanings and whether or not they have relevance today, since some date from long ago.

The students are asked in various exercises to debate, brainstorm, or role play. These techniques are described below.

Debate is to engage in a formal discussion or argument. Debating provides an opportunity to discuss opposing points of view. It is helpful to clarify the purpose of debating to students. They need to appreciate the difference between fighting and discussing different points of view and the benefits of discussion. Point out that there is not necessarily a right or wrong, but that often responsible citizens can have different opinions on a topic. Point out that people are not good or bad, or right or wrong, or your enemies if they disagree with you.

Brainstorm is defined as a sudden, clever, whimsical, or foolish idea. Brainstorming is a chance for students to let their brains be free from constraint and to express whatever thoughts or ideas come to mind without critical evaluation or judgment. This encourages free expression and hopefully many creative, fresh, and new ideas will emerge.

Role playing is a technique best used when students are divided into small groups of four or five. Shy students should be mixed with students who would be good catalysts. Students should establish as much background about the situation or the character in the role play as possible. The more specific the background facts, the more effective the role play. Encourage students to switch roles in order for them to better understand various viewpoints. Script writing of role plays is helpful in developing writing skills.

GA1327

Chapter 1

What Is Citizenship?

"Citizenship is man's basic right, for it is nothing less than his right to have rights."

Chief Justice Earl Warren, 1958

GA1327

Introduction

Get ready. Your adventure is about to begin. First, always complete Word Play so that you will be prepared to conquer any new words you meet along your way.

Now close your eyes and imagine you have just awakened to find you are the only person left in the universe! Try to imagine this. You are free from many rules and responsibilities!

But, in this book, you are not alone for long. As you are joined by others, you will learn about the necessity of building a community with laws and ethics that will protect and help you and others who live together. You will better understand why the rules and responsibilities you did not need when alone are so important now. You will appreciate the many privileges and rights you have as a member of your community and the role you must play as a citizen living with other citizens.

"You cannot make yourself feel something you do not feel, but you can make yourself do right in spite of your feelings."

Paul S. Bucks, 1967

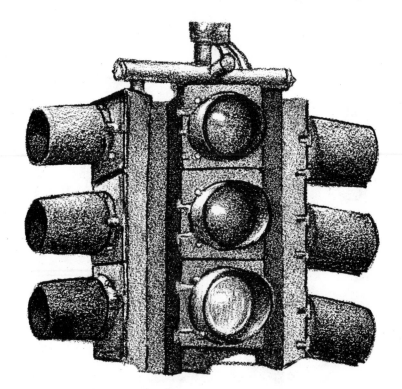

2

GA1327

Word Play

Unscramble the following words and look up their meanings. You will find each of these words in the chapter.

toncciv _____

Meaning: _____

ttesrop _____

Meaning: _____

rruoctpnoi _____

Meaning: _____

qlauyite _____

Meaning: _____

pporaandag _____

Meaning: _____

noinu _____

Meaning: _____

tlaassu _____

Meaning: _____

gtnriesspas _____

Meaning: _____

fitnediaciniot _____

Meaning: _____

rionnvetemnsilat _____

Meaning: _____

ratotmneocm _____

Meaning: _____

cioatonisas _____

Meaning: _____

iivrpgeel _____

Meaning: _____

ncosttietu _____

Meaning: _____

ttiepnoi _____

Meaning: _____

Unscrambled Words

environmentalist	union	propaganda	identification
convict	corruption	commentator	privilege
assault	association	petition	trespassing
protest	equality	constitute	

GA1327

Alone

Imagine you are the only person left in the universe. Which of the following behaviors would no longer be necessary and why? Circle those behaviors and explain your reason on the lines that follow.

Keeping quiet after 10 p.m. _____

_____

Keeping the streets, rivers, and oceans free of litter. _____

_____

No trespassing. _____

_____

Catching a limit of three fish a day. _____

_____

Keeping healthy and fit. _____

_____

Stopping at all stop signs and red lights. _____

_____

Discuss with your teacher and classmates the behaviors you've circled and your reasons. Discuss together if something like making loud noise after midnight is inherently "wrong" if only you exist.

4

GA1327

We're Free!
No More Rules and Reponsibilities

Continue to imagine that you are the only person left in the universe. Make a list of all the rules and responsibilities that you once needed but would no longer need.

Rules and responsibilities at school:

_____

_____

_____

_____

Rules and responsibilities at home:

_____

_____

_____

_____

Rules and responsibilities in your neighborhood:

_____

_____

_____

_____

Rules and responsibilities with friends:

_____

_____

_____

_____

Discuss with your teacher and classmates why these rules and responsibilities once were important and no longer are. Now you can begin to understand that when you live with others in a city or community you are a citizen. A citizen has rights, privileges, and duties. These rights, privileges, and duties wouldn't exist if you happened to be the only person in your universe or community.

Creating a Community

Now imagine that you are no longer alone in your universe. You are joined with other people once again, and you all live together in one large area. You call this a community. A community can be as small as your family or as large as the world. People who have things in common form communities—the commonalities can be social, professional, recreational, economic, etc. A member of a community is called a citizen. A citizen has rights, privileges, and duties, as we have already discovered.

The citizens in the community have been busy building. Explain why each of the following items has become a necessary part of the community.

four-way stop signs _____

identification cards _____

fire hydrants _____

fences _____

List ten other items that were not necessary when you were alone but are necessary now that you are living with others. Explain the necessity of each.

_____

_____

_____

_____

_____

_____

_____

_____

_____

_____

_____

GA1327

Building My Community

Draw and color your new community below. Be sure to include all the items and buildings that are necessary now that you live with others. Using clay, papier-mâché, or cardboard, make a display of your community for your classroom. Also mention community leaders that will be needed.

"Tis the people, not the houses, that make the city."

Thomas Fuller, 1732

7

Acting Like a Citizen

Follow the directions below.

Laws or Rules
Name a situation or time when you'd get in trouble if you talked.

_____

_____

Free Choice
Name a situation or time in which you would be free to *talk* any time you wanted.

_____

_____

Social Responsibilities
Name a situation or time in which you would be free to *talk*, but it would be better not to.

_____

_____

Using the examples you have just written, discuss with your teacher and classmates the differences between obeying a law or rule, behaving responsibly, and choosing freely. Human action includes all three types of behavior. Laws are made to be obeyed. At the opposite end of the scale, some choices may be made freely. In free choice, the law has no say: attending a basketball game, taking up a new hobby, and choosing a new friend are examples. Between the two ends of the scale is an area in which a citizen has certain responsibilities, even though there are no laws to obey. Examples of things in this area include manners and ethics. It is not against the law to cut in line in the grocery story, but most citizens would not do this anyway. Choosing to stand in line is therefore an act of *citizenship*.

Laws and Rules   **Social Responsibilities**   **Free Choice**

   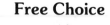

"No man is above the law and no man below it; nor do we ask any man's permission when we require him to obey it. Obedience to the law is demanded as a right; not asked as a favor."

Theodore Roosevelt, 1903

What About You?

Read and answer the following questions:

What is a law or rule you must obey when playing with your friends?

_____

What are you free to do when you are playing with your friends?

_____

What would you never do with friends even though there is no rule or law against this?

_____

Name five things you can think of that you would get in trouble doing.

_____

_____

_____

_____

_____

Name five things you can think of that you are always free to do.

_____

_____

_____

_____

_____

Name five things you can think of that you would never do even though there is no rule or law against it. Explain your reason.

_____

_____

_____

_____

_____

                                                     GA1327

The Matching Game

Citizenship is the empowerment of an individual with the rights, privileges, and duties of a citizen. Being a citizen means obeying laws which are created in order to help people live together, exercising the right of free choice to make independent decisions, and being socially responsible in situations where there are no laws to obey. This sense of duty or responsibility comes from peoples' ethics, values, and morals. But keep in mind that peoples' social responsibilities also vary in different cultures.

Citizenship includes peoples' responsibilities to do something about the things they find unsatisfactory. Citizens must decide if the rules are good ones. If not, citizens have responsibilities to exercise their rights to change the government's laws and rules.

Now, using what you have just learned in this exercise, match Column A and Column B by drawing lines.

Column A	Column B
Law	stopping at a traffic light
	choosing a person to marry
	helping an elderly person to cross the street
	paying taxes
Free Choice	choosing a place to vacation
	not littering
	trying to get more shelter for the homeless
Social Responsibility	standing in line waiting for a bus
	not speaking when someone else is speaking
	not speaking to people who get on the elevator
Fighting for Social Change	selling your house
	signing a petition in order to close down a town dump

10

Power for the People

Read the article below and answer the questions that follow.

A Lesson in the Power of the People

Arizona is offering America a rare lesson in the power of citizens to challenge their leaders. Angry Arizonians by the thousands want to oust their governor, Evan Mecham, before his term ends in 1991.

In 1986, Mecham, a Republican, won election with a minority of the vote. The bulk of ballots were split between two Democratic opponents. But Mecham had hardly settled into office when outraged citizens were demanding his ouster. The spark that ignited the fight was Mecham's overturning of Jan. 15 as a state holiday honoring Dr. Martin Luther King, Jr., the civil-rights leader who was assassinated in 1968.

Mecham said that former Gov. Bruce Babbit's declaration of the holiday was illegal. Only the legislature can authorize holidays and it had refused to do so. But Mecham didn't help his cause when he said that King wasn't worth a holiday.

His remarks on other issues fueled the fire. Gay-rights groups fumed when he said homosexuals don't have civil rights. Others opposed a planned $50 million cut in the education budget. Some of Mecham's appointees were seen as unqualified for their jobs. And there was the matter of a $350,000 campaign loan he failed to declare.

But what could opponents do?

Under Arizona law, voters can force a special "recall" election. Mecham's opponents had to gather, on petitions, voters' signatures equalling 25 percent of the votes cast in the last gubernatorial election—in this case, 216,746 votes.

More than 300,000 signatures were collected. After Jan. 18, Gov. Mecham has five days to decide whether or not to quit. If he refuses, a recall election, pitting him against other candidates, must be held between May 12 and June 13.

Only one other state governor has ever been recalled. North Dakota voters did it 67 years ago. Will history repeat itself?

—Peter M. Jones[1]

Questions

1. Find at least two words you do not know the meanings of in the article above. Underline in red these words and look them up in your own dictionary.

2. What kind of change are these citizens fighting for and why?

   _____

   _____

3. How did these citizens use the law to help them get the change they wanted?

   _____

   _____

4. How do you feel about citizens having the power to challenge their leaders? Do you think this is helpful or harmful to a community and why?

   _____

   _____

5. What kind of social change do you think is necessary in your school community? Neighborhood? What would you be willing to do about it? Discuss with your teacher and classmates.

   _____

   _____

[1]From Scholastic UPDATE. Copyright © 1988 by Scholastic Inc. All rights reserved.

Civil Yet Disobedient?
What Is Civil Disobedience?

Follow the directions below.

Look in the glossary for the definition of *civil*. Write it below.

_____

Look in the glossary for the definition of *disobedience*. Write it below.

_____

Together with your teacher and classmates, write a definition of *civil disobedience* below by putting the two definitions together.

_____

_____

_____

Now look up in your glossary the definition of *civil disobedience*. Write it below. Compare it to the definition you and your classmates created.

_____

_____

_____

Together with your teacher and classmates think of five examples of civil disobedience. Write them below.

_____

_____

_____

_____

GA1327

Is This or Is This Not Civil Disobedience?

Look over the list of words below. Find the definitions in your own dictionary of any word(s) of which you do not know the meaning.

kidnap, demonstration, looting, picket, riot, terrorism, boycott, swindle, sit-in, counterfeit, strike, propaganda

Violence is defined as physical force exerted for the purpose of violating, damaging or abusing.

Civil disobedience is defined as the refusal to obey certain governmental laws or demands for the purpose of influencing government policy. It is characterized by nonviolent techniques as boycotting and picketing.

Now circle in green actions that describe civil disobedience. Circle in red actions that do not describe civil disobedience.

Discuss with your teacher and classmates the difference between *civil disobedience* and *violence*.

Mr. J kidnaps the daughter of a well-known news commentator because the news he is reporting is creating racial tension in his community. Mr. J believes in social equality and wants this propaganda stopped.

A group of environmentalists tie themselves to trees as a way to stop the city from cutting down the trees.

Hospital workers go on strike for two weeks in order to get better pay and fight for better working conditions in the hospital.

A bomb is placed in the car of a judge because a group of citizens are angry at the judge's decision not to convict a man who the community believes has sexually assaulted young children.

Citizens write and print an underground newspaper in order to spread important information that the city is trying to keep secret. The citizens feel that keeping this information a secret will lead to big problems in their community.

Citizens march on the grounds of the White House protesting a decision to make abortion illegal.

A crowd of demonstrators decide to destroy the mayor's property as a way of showing the authorities they would no longer tolerate the cutback in funding for public housing.

Citizens form a secret association in order to try to stop corruption within their labor union.

13
GA1327

Demonstrating an Opinion

Look through your weekly or daily newspaper. Cut out and paste below an article describing a boycott, picket, strike, march or demonstration. If you need more room, tape the article to a blank sheet of paper.

Write three of your own opinions about what is taking place. Then ask a classmate to read your article and write three of his/her opinions. Write those below. Compare, discuss, and debate your opinions on the issues.

Example:

1980

JULY-SEPTEMBER: Workers at the Lenin Shipyard in Gdansk, Poland, strike for better pay and working conditions. The government grants workers the right to form a trade union, Solidarity. The union is headed by Lech Walesa, a Gdansk shipyard worker.

From Scholastic UPDATE. Copyright © 1989 by Scholastic Inc. All rights reserved.

My Opinions
1. I think it is good that citizens strike to try to get what they deserve.
2. Unions will help protect the workers.
3. The citizens are making themselves heard by striking and that is important.

Classmates' Opinions
1. I don't think it is a good idea to have unions. More problems occur for the community.
2. The citizens are asking for too much.
3. Citizens are finding a good way to make their complaints known.

Paste your article below.

Your Opinions

1. _____

_____

_____

2. _____

_____

_____

3. _____

_____

Classmates' Opinions

1. _____

_____

_____

2. _____

_____

_____

3. _____

_____

GA1327

Citizens' Rights

Write on these citizens' signs those things which you believe every citizen should have a right to.

Examples are education, health care, free speech, respect.

Discuss with your teacher and classmates the rights you would fight for and why.

"It is fair to judge peoples by the rights they will sacrifice most for."

Clarence Day, 1920

"I am the inferior of any man whose rights I trample underfoot."

Robert G. Ingersoll, 1884

GA1327

Balancing the Scales

See how many scales you can balance by filling in the blanks.

What are your privileges in the community you live in?

1. _____
2. _____
3. _____

What are your duties in the community you live in?

1. _____
2. _____
3. _____

What are your privileges in your school?

1. _____
2. _____
3. _____

What are your duties to your school?

1. _____
2. _____
3. _____

"What men value in this world is not rights but privileges."

H.Z. Mercker, 1956

GA1327

More Scales to Balance

Balance the scales by filling in the blanks.

What are your privileges in your environment?

1. _____
2. _____
3. _____

What are your duties to your environment?

1. _____
2. _____
3. _____

What are your privileges to your family?

1. _____
2. _____
3. _____

What are your duties to your family?

1. _____
2. _____
3. _____

Discuss with your teacher and classmates which circumstances you give more to and which you get more from. Do your scales need to be better balanced? If so, what can you do in order to create a better balance?

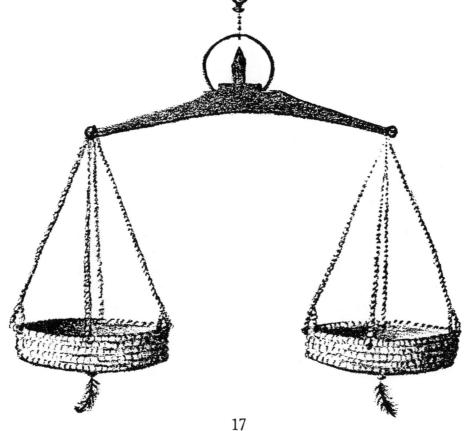

GA1327

"This Land Is Your Land, This Land Is My Land"

Imagine growing up in one country and then moving and living in another. We call people who leave a country to settle permanently in another immigrants. To immigrate means to enter and settle in a country to which one is not a native. Discuss with your teacher and classmates what you imagine the hardships would be in being an immigrant? The rewards? Obstacles to overcome?

Below two well-known American immigrants write a few words about their experiences as immigrants. These excerpts came from *The Wall Street Journal*, Tuesday, July 3rd, 1990.*

Henry Kaufman
Economist
Born: Wenings, Germany—1927
Naturalized: New York—1942

I came to America when I was 10 years old. The question before my family had been whether to leave our comfortable, middle-class existence and cross the ocean to the unknown. The decision was made for us one night when, following a torchlight parade, the Nazis broke into our house.

Shortly after our arrival, I went to the local public school. The principal tried to evaluate my English-language skills. He pointed to his hand, fingers and nose and I responded by saying the correct words because they were the same in German. Of course, he quickly realized that I did not know any English at all. I was put in the first grade, where I was the oldest and the tallest child.

Going to college was assumed as a matter of course by my parents. Because of the burden this would pose for them, I pushed hard to complete my undergraduate work in 2½ years and then took just one year to qualify for a master's degree. I earned my Ph.D. at night over seven years while I held a full-time job. Later, I was fortunate that Charles Simon, a partner at Salomon Brothers, recognized my work. He introduced me to Sidney Homer, of the bond market research department, who gave me my first job there.

Alex Kozinski
Judge—Court of Appeals, Ninth Circuit
Born: Bucharest, Romania—1950
Naturalized: Los Angeles—1968

Learning English for everyday use was one thing; mastering its nuances was quite another. Matters were complicated by the fact that my primary connection to American culture was the TV and endless hours of "The Andy Griffith Show," "Father Knows Best," "The Donna Reed Show" and "Leave It to Beaver." Were real American families like that?

I got my chance to find out when a schoolmate, Andrew Reineke, invited me home for dinner. Was this my chance to meet Ward, June and Wally Cleaver? With some apprehension, I accepted. No little Jewish boy with a thick Romanian accent had ever shown up in Mayberry; there was no script for this episode. I would have to wing it.

Andrew and I found Mr. Reineke in the rec room. "Tell me, Alex," he asked, "why did your family come to America?" I've heard that question a thousand times, but I've never figured out how to answer it. How do you explain the obvious? "Are you pushing my leg, sir?" I replied. "We came to America for the same reaosn as everyone—because we could."

At dinner, after grace, plates of food were passed around "American style," as I had seen on television. I was helping myself to mashed potatoes when Mr. Reineke confronted me with a fateful question: "Would you like a glass of milk?"

"No, thank you, ma'am. I don't drink," I heard myself answering. Had I just claimed to be a teetotaler or a camel? I attempted a tactical retreat: "What I meant to say is that we have plenty of milk at home."

"So, what do you plan to do?" Mr. Reineke growled, "run home between courses?"

After reading these people's experiences, what appreciations do you have for immigrants?

_____

Any resentments? _____

How would you feel as an immigrant? _____

If you were an immigrant, what would you imagine wanting from the citizens of your new country?

_____

"Our Constitution is founded on the principle that all men are equal as citizens and entitled to the same rights, whether they achieved citizenship by birth, or after coming here as immigrants, seeking to find in America new freedom and new opportunities."

John F. Kennedy, 1960

*Reprinted with permission of *The Wall Street Journal*, copyright 1990, Dow Jones and Company, Inc. All rights reserved.

18

Becoming a Citizen

Write a story about one of the two topics below.

1. A young boy and girl and their family travel from another country to the United States. Eventually they all become United States citizens. Write a story about their travels, their experiences, adventures, obstacles, hopes, dreams, and disappointments. Describe step by step what they do to become citizens of the U.S. Before writing the story, write to the nearest office of the U.S. Immigration and Naturalization Service to find out how people with other citizenship can become citizens of the U.S.

2. Choose a country other than the United States which interests you. Go to your library and/or contact the embassies or consulates of the country you selected. Find out how to become a citizen of the country you have chosen. Try to find someone from that country who lives near you. Find out what that person has to say about the country you have chosen. Report your findings to your class.

GA1327

Chapter 2

What Attitudes and Actions Lead to Responsible Citizenship?

"We uniformally applaud what is right and condemn what is wrong when it costs us nothing but the sentiment."

William Hazlitt, 1823

Introduction

Chapter 2 digs deeper into the actions and attitudes which underlie concepts of responsible citizenship. Some of these include helpfulness, responsibility, respect, and involvement. In this chapter you will gain more understanding of how your own values and attitudes influence your views as a citizen. Be prepared to experience changes in yourself as some of your actions, attitudes, values, and beliefs become consciously known to you for the first time. The feelings you experience are part of your process of personal growth and change. The capacity to change will be an asset to you throughout your life. Try to build personal skill at being able to change.

GA1327

Word Play

Find the vocabulary words hidden in the maze, circle them and write their definitions below. Have fun!

```
V O L U N T E E R C P A R Q R
A K O P S H O P L I F T C B A
L P R C U V U N J U S T Q U H
U E V I T A L I T Y F I Z A C
E N B D E B R A I N S T O R M
S A H J L S S U W N X U H F L
T L K I T C H N E A R D L Y N
A T C O N S C I E N C E M D R
J Y I N I T I A T I V E R S I
```

Words to Find in Your Own Dictionary

volunteer _____

unjust _____

initiative _____

attitude _____

conscience _____

vitality _____

penalty _____

shoplift _____

values _____

brainstorm _____

22

Find Gumdrops' Path Out

Gumdrops is trying to find her way out of the maze. Help Gumdrops to find the only path out by finding the attitudes and actions that are on the path to responsible citizenship.

Follow the path to the next page and continue this activity.

GA1327

Find the Path to Responsible Citizenship

Now design your own maze and have each path lead to responsible citizenship. Change each of the dead-end attitudes and actions (from the activity on the previous page) into responsible citizenship attitudes and actions.

Discuss with your teacher and classmates how the attitudes and actions you chose can help lead to responsible citizenship. How would you define *responsible citizenship*? What is a responsible citizen?

GA1327

Freedom and Responsibility

"Those who expect to reap the blessings of freedom must, like men, undergo the fatigue of supporting it."

Thomas Paine

Try to understand why citizens cannot have friends without responsibility as you do the following activity.

Imagine that your school has a policy that all food must be thrown in the garbage after eating lunch in your cafeteria. Now imagine that most students do not pay attention to this policy and leave food on the tables and floors. So now imagine that the school imposes a stricter policy since students are not acting responsibly. This policy says anyone caught leaving food on the floors or tables will be suspended. Now imagine that most students still ignore this policy although many students are being suspended. So now imagine the school imposes an even stricter policy which does not allow them to leave the cafeteria until each one is escorted to the garbage can with his tray. No student is free to leave the cafeteria until everyone has been escorted to the garbage can.

Why have the students lost their freedom? _____

If they acted responsibly, would they have less restrictions imposed on them? Why?

_____

Discuss and explain.

Acting responsibly as citizens allows for more freedom. Freedom without responsibility can lead to anarchy. Anarchy is when citizens do whatever they want without regard for the concerns, feelings, or interests of others. What do you think might have happened if students continued not to follow any policy and the authorities didn't do anything about it? Do you think there was a need for stricter rules?

Below are two of the many freedoms United States' citizens are granted. List citizens' responsibilities toward these freedoms.

Freedom of Speech
Citizens' responsibilities include defending others' rights to freedom whether or not citizens agree with what is being said.

Freedom of Worship
Citizens' responsibilities include religious tolerance.

"We are in bondage to the law so that we may be free."

Marcus Cicero

25

GA1327

To Obey or Not to Obey

Below are listed various types of governments and how they operate. Discuss the differences with your teacher and classmates and decide how free and how responsible citizens are under each form of government. Write the type of government somewhere on the scale below to describe how free and how responsible citizens are.

Democracy—Ninety percent of adult citizens vote regularly in elections.

Republic—Twenty-seven percent of adult citizens vote regularly in elections.

Dictatorship—An army general controls the civilian police.

Anarchy—Each citizen does what he or she wants without regard for the concerns, feelings, or interests of others.

X. Country in which no single group maintains control. People who wish to travel between regions do so at the discretion of local militia leaders.

Y. Country in which no one wants the local money because it is worthless. People work several jobs, smuggle, and prefer foreign money or precious metal as payment in transactions.

Freedom
without
responsibility

Freedom and
responsibility

Little freedom,
little responsibility

Research and find out which countries in the world practice democracy or have dictatorships, etc. See how many countries' governments you can identify.

"Intellectual freedom is essential to human society. Freedom of thought is the only guarantee against an infection of people by mass myths, which, in the hands of treacherous hypocrites and demagogues, can be transformed into bloody dictatorships."

Andrei Sakharov

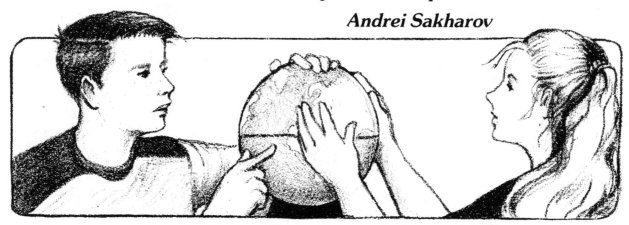

GA1327

Four Corners

This activity is a class activity. Students should stand together in the center of the room. The teacher will read aloud the situations below. Each student should decide his/her sense of responsibility for the outcome and stand in the corner of the room labelled accordingly. One corner will read *fully responsible*, another *as responsible as the person who did it*, another *partly responsible* and another *not responsible at all*. Each student should then explain his position. Discussion and debate should follow. Those students who choose the corner which reads *not at all responsible* should state who they believe is responsible.

1. You introduce one of your school friends to your new neighbor who moved into the house across the street. They become good friends and end up breaking a neighbor's window while trespassing on his property. How responsible are you?

2. You and your friends are eating lunch in the cafeteria. Suddenly a food fight begins. The kids from the table behind you begin throwing oranges, squirting ketchup, and throwing their hot dogs. You join in and dump a glass of ice water down your friend's back. Just before the principal arrives, one of your classmates gets seriously injured by a flying fork which hits him in the head. He has to be taken to the hospital. How responsible are you for his injury?

3. Your father is sexually and physically abusive with your younger sister. You are the only one who knows this, and you have been told not to ever tell anyone. Your sister ends up injured after your father's violent rampage one night. How responsible are you for your sister's injuries?

Now divide into three groups. Each group role-plays one of the above situations using responsible citizenship skills so that the crime, tragedy, or injury is prevented.

To be a responsible citizen, I must remember _____

_____

_____

_____

GA1327

Who Am I?

Read the following cartoon strips. Decide the character in each cartoon who reacts most like you would in the same situation. Circle that character and describe the attitudes you share with the character on the lines below the cartoon.

1st Cartoon

_____

_____

_____

2nd Cartoon

_____

_____

_____

3rd Cartoon

_____

_____

_____

Discuss with your teacher and classmates the attitudes and actions which most resemble your own. Discuss how you feel about your attitudes and if you think that they reflect responsible citizenship. If not, discuss the attitudes which do.

Use the cartoons above to complete the activity on the page that follows.

GA1327

Evaluating Reactions

Look at cartoon 3 again and answer the following questions.

1. Rate the characters from 1 to 5 as to whose behaviors you think reflect the best values to the worst values. Use a number 1 to represent the best behavior and number 5 the worst. Explain your thoughts about each.

2. If it was your own dog, would you have responded the same way you did to someone else's dog? Why or why not? Your best friend's dog? Your worst enemy's dog? Explain.

_____

_____

_____

Look at cartoon 2 again and answer the following questions.

3. Imagine you are the classmate that gossips behind her back. What might you be feeling to act the way you do?
   - Gossiping makes you feel you are better than the loser.
   - Gossiping makes you feel important, like you know things that other people don't know.
   - Gossiping is your way of feeling close to others. It gives you something to talk to others about.
   - Gossiping is a way to get back at others.

   Imagine that you are the classmate who tries to cheer her up by telling jokes. What might you be feeling to act this way?
   - Telling jokes when someone is sad is your way of not having to feel sadness.
   - Telling jokes when someone is sad is your way to keep up your image of being the happy person who always makes people feel good.

   Imagine you are the classmate that doesn't get the part in the play. What are you feeling when someone puts his arms around you?
   - You feel it is okay to be sad and disappointed and cry.
   - You feel cared about.
   - You feel like you matter.
   - You feel embarrassed.
   - You feel like a baby.

4. Why do you think others walk away from situations? Why do you think others laugh at people who are in bad situations?

   Have you ever been laughed at when you were in an embarrassing or bad situation? How did it make you feel? How did you feel about the other person?

   Have you ever laughed at someone who was in an embarrassing situation or a bad situation? How do you think the other person felt? Explain.

GA1327

What's Enough for You?

How involved or uninvolved are you? Read each situation and draw yourself on the rung of the ladder that describes your level of involvement.

Your class is planning a dance. You would most likely . . .

Rung 5	go to the dance and help hang up coats, help advertise the event, and help with all preparations.
Rung 4	go to the dance and help hang up coats and help advertise the event.
Rung 3	go to the dance as well as help hang up coats.
Rung 2	go to the dance.
Rung 1	not go to the dance.

Students, including yourself, are angry at the sexist attitudes in your new textbook. You would most likely . . .

Rung 5	organize a group of students to fight to switch textbooks and complain to teachers and administration and get your parents involved and get classmates to do something.
Rung 4	complain to your teachers and administrators and get your parents involved and encourage other classmates to do something.
Rung 3	get your parents to speak to the teachers and encourage other classmates to do something.
Rung 2	not do anything except encourage others to do something.
Rung 1	not do anything.

Discuss with your teacher and classmates how involved or uninvolved you usually become. Do you typically wait for others to get involved while you sit back, or do you get actively involved? Are you comfortable with your level of involvement? Is it helpful to you? To others?

GA1327

Enough Is Enough!

Read each scenario below. Then write what is enough to do considering the question of what actions lead to being a responsible citizen.

a. Alice got a soda from a machine.
   When she was finished she threw the can on the ground.
   Is it enough to pay for what you drink, or should you also throw the container way?
   Is it enough to throw your container away, or should you also pick up other people's trash?
   Is it enough to pick up other people's trash, or should you also tell them not to litter?
   Is it enough to tell other people not to litter, or should you report them as well?
   Is it enough to report them, or should you also make sure the police or authorities did their job?

   It is enough to _____

b. John and his friends experiment with drugs and alcohol.
   Should John experiment with drugs and alcohol or choose not to even if his friends choose to experiment?
   Is it enough for John not to experiment, or should he also try to convince his friends not to experiment with drugs and alcohol?
   Is it enough for him to try to convince his friends not to experiment, or should he also not hang out with them?
   Is it enough for John not to hang out with his friends, or should he also report them to the authorities?

   It is enough to _____

c. Lawson sees a crime out his window.
   Is it enough that he report the crime to the police, or should he also scream something out the window?
   Is it enough to scream something out the window, or should he also go out and try to intervene, until the police arrive?
   Is it enough for Lawson to intervene, or should he also make sure at some point in the future to unite neighbors to patrol the streets and help stamp out the crime?

   It is enough to _____

Discuss with your teacher and classmates what is enough when trying to be a responsible citizen. Discuss and debate your ideas with one another.

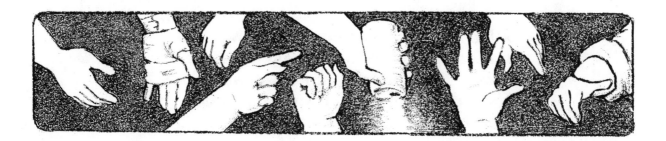

GA1327

Respect

Respect is an essential ingredient to being a responsible citizen. What is respect and how is it developed? Answer the questions below.

> Respect is defined as a feeling of regard and honor.

Draw a picture of the person or persons you most respect. Make sure you draw him wearing a big top hat and an oversized T-shirt. On his hat and T-shirt write all the qualities the person(s) possesses that you respect (for example: able to stay calm in tense situations).

Now draw a picture of yourself. Make sure you draw yourself wearing a big top hat and an oversized T-shirt. On your hat and T-shirt write all the qualities you possess that you respect about yourself (for example: I'm a good listener). Ask classmates to add what they respect about you on your T-shirt and hat.

A teacher, noticing how courteous and polite one of her pupils was, wished to praise her and teach the class a lesson. She asked, "Who taught you to be so polite?" The girl laughed and answered, "Really, no one. It just runs in our family."

GA1327

What Would You Do?

Write down what you would do in each of the following situations.

You are walking through the park with a group of your friends. One friend picks up a stone and throws it against a fence. Another friend does the same. Then all of your friends start collecting stones trying to knock down the fence. What do you do and why?

_____

_____

_____

Your neighborhood is using whistle blowing as a way of preventing street crime in your community. Each person carries a whistle. If anyone sees a crime or a victim of a crime, he is to blow his whistle. If someone hears a whistle being blown, he is to blow his own. You and your friends are walking down the street. Just for fun your friends blow their whistles. What do you do and why?

_____

_____

_____

Your teacher sends you up to the school storage room to get supplies. You look around the room and see many art and gym supplies that you'd love to have. As a matter of fact, you've been trying to save your allowance in order to buy some of these things. You realize no one would ever know if you stole these supplies. What do you do and why?

_____

_____

_____

Based on your responses to these situations, how respectful are you? Discuss with your teacher and classmates what your responses have to do with respect and if your ability to respect others' rights and property is respectable.

GA1327

Respect as Citizens

As citizens we must develop respect for ourselves and for others, as well as respect for laws and our environment. Under each column write the specific ways you show respect.

How I show respect for

Laws   **My Environment**

Myself   **Neighbors**

Discuss new and different ways you can show respect to yourself, your neighbors, your environment, and the laws. Are there any ways in which you are disrespectful? What can you do to change these behaviors? Discuss.

Discuss the following quote by Martin Luther King and try to understand what he meant by it. Do you agree or disagree? Explain.

"I submit that an individual who breaks a law that conscience tells him is unjust and willingly accepts the penalty by staying in jail to raise the conscience of the community over its injustice is in reality expressing the very highest respect for law."

Martin Luther King, 1964

GA1327

Being Left Out

Developing an attitude of including others is helpful to being a responsible citizen.

Think of all the times you remember being left out. Write each below and include how it made you feel.

Being Left Out   **How I Felt**

Now remember times you've left out others. Write them below and include your reasons and how you imagine the person or persons to have felt.

Leaving Others Out   **Reason**   **Persons' Feelings**

Now look over your list of reasons. Are there any good reasons to leave people out?

What are they? _____ _____ _____

Which reasons are excuses? _____ _____ _____

When is it okay to leave people out? _____

When is it not? _____

Discuss with your teacher and classmates.

What messages did you receive from your parents about leaving others out? (For example: It's okay if the person is different from you.)

_____

What messages did you receive from the media (magazines, TV, videos) about leaving others out? _____

Which of these messages (from parents and media) do you agree with and which do you not agree with? _____

What message do you want to give to yourself? _____

                                                   GA1327

I Would . . .

A new girl moves into the house next door to you. She wants to be friendly with you, and she doesn't know any other kids in town or in school. She feels very lonely and left out.

Consider each of the cases below separately. For each case, write down how you would react.

You don't like the way her hair or the clothes she wears look. She seems different from the friends you hang around with.

_____

_____

_____

_____

Your parents have always discouraged you from being friendly with people from other religious backgrounds, and this girl is different.

_____

_____

_____

_____

You like her but your friends don't like her and warn you if you hang out with her, they won't have anything to do with you.

_____

_____

_____

_____

She is very athletic, smart, and popular with the boys, and this is threatening to you.

_____

_____

_____

_____

Discuss with your teacher and classmates your reactions, and together determine which ones reflect being a responsible citizen.

GA1327

Thinking Helpfully

Thinking helpfully is another ingredient in being a responsible citizen.

I feel like I want to be helpful most when _____.

It is most difficult for me to be helpful when _____.

Asking others for help is easiest for me when _____.

Asking others for help is most difficult for me when _____.

It is easier for me to (ask for help/be helpful) because _____.

Describe a time you remember when someone helped you out. How did you feel?

_____

Describe a time when you helped someone else out. How did you feel? _____

_____

. . . .

Have a contest with your classmates. See who can come up with the longest list of ways to be helpful in the following places or situations. You have four minutes for each one. On your mark, get set, go!

All the ways I could be helpful in my classroom:

All the ways I could be helpful to an elderly neighbor:

All the ways I could be helpful in my neighborhood:

All the ways I could be helpful in keeping the air clean:

All the ways I could be helpful in raising money for cancer research:

All the ways I could be helpful at the scene of an accident in which I am not involved:

GA1327

Help!

Learning to be helpful is an important ingredient in being a responsible citizen.

Read each situation below. Identify what it would take for you to be helpful.

A classmate needs someone to carry his books because he is on crutches.

- ☐ I would refuse.
- ☐ I would offer my help.
- ☐ I would carry his books only if the teacher made me.
- ☐ I would carry his books only if he was one of the popular kids.
- ☐ I would carry his books only if he paid me.
- ☐ I would carry his books because it is the right thing to do.

A neighbor asks you to help him rake his leaves.

- ☐ I would refuse no matter what.
- ☐ I would offer him my help.
- ☐ I would offer him my help only if I was not busy.
- ☐ I would help him only if I had nothing better to do.
- ☐ I would help him only if he paid me at least $3.00 per hour.
- ☐ I would help him only if he couldn't find anyone else.
- ☐ I would help so my neighbor's would like me.

There is a water shortage. You are asked to help conserve water.

- ☐ I would refuse no matter what.
- ☐ I would conserve water only when others are watching.
- ☐ I would conserve water only if I would get in trouble if I didn't.
- ☐ I would conserve water only if they paid me.
- ☐ I would conserve water no matter what.

Discuss with your teacher and classmates the conditions under which you are willing to be helpful. Decide how you feel about your helpfulness and share this aloud. If you are not satisfied with your helpfulness, decide what you would like to change. Discuss with your classmates specific changes you can make this week.

GA1327

Wanting and Needing

Knowing what we need and want is helpful to being a responsible citizen.

Color the mosaic using the key below.

Blue—things I need to survive
Orange—things I want but could live without
Green—things I don't want or need

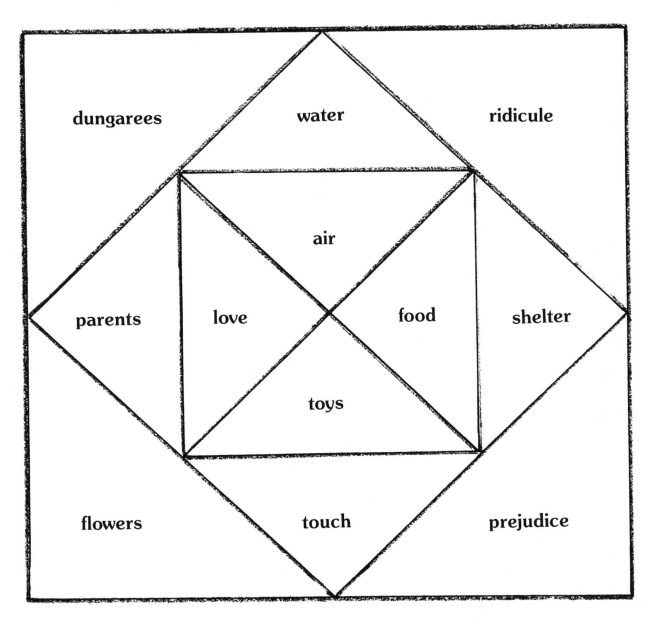

Needs are essential to our survival, strength, and vitality. *Wants* make our lives easier and more pleasant. Some things are a threat to our survival or enjoyment. Discuss with your teacher and classmates how each of the items written above is either essential to your survival, a threat to it, or an added luxury. We usually value our *needs* most since we cannot exist without those (food, water). Discuss which of your needs and/or wants is satisfied or unsatisfied. How does that feel to you?

GA1327

Helping Where Needed

Like individuals, communities have needs. When a community's needs are being met, the community is strong and full of confidence and vitality. Much of the community's strength and vitality arises from the *initiative and concern* of its citizens.

If a community's needs go unmet, the community suffers from problems, and its members may become negative, fearful, and unhappy. Often a community with unmet needs is one in which the citizens show indifference toward other people's needs, and expect others to meet the community's needs.

With your teacher and classmates, brainstorm a list of the unmet needs in your community. Then divide into groups of four. Each group chooses four unmet needs from the class list and thinks of ways that volunteers could be helpful in meeting these needs.

In your group, choose at least one of your four unmet needs. Help organize committees to enlist volunteers to begin meeting this need in your community.

Unmet Needs **Volunteer Services**
For example: need more dogcatchers   help the local animal shelter

Try to notice the needs and wants of those around you in your home or school community. For example, notice that your classmate John seems to need a lot of encouragement. Make note of this and each day find ways to encourage him. Or, notice that your sister could use more time to study. Volunteer some of your time to help her complete her chores so she can have more time for her studies. List below the needs or unmet needs of those around you.

GA1327

Volunteer to Be a Detective

Pretend you are a detective. Use all your detective skills to uncover the following information. First, uncover the definition of a *volunteer*.

Uncover situations in your community where people are being good citizens by being volunteers. See how many you can find.

For example: Little League soccer coach

Citizens in your community have needs, some of which are being addressed by these volunteers. Identify the needs that are being addressed.

For example: the need children have for adults to help them organize sporting events

From all the types of needs and volunteer activities you've identified, write the ones you would and would not want to volunteer for.

Would   **Would Not**

Choose one volunteer activity from your Would column and find out the address, telephone number, person to contact and how you could be helpful.

Discuss with your teacher and classmates what the advantages and disadvantages would be if your community had no volunteers. If you had only volunteers.

41 GA1327

Responsible Citizen's Recipe

Here are some of the ingredients we've discovered that create responsible citizens. Think of other ingredients (attitudes and values, traits and qualities) and add them to our recipe. Then write the rest of the recipe's directions.

Cooking Up Responsible Citizens

3 dashes of helpfulness
2 cups of respect
sprinkle in responsibility
6 teaspoons of involvement

Add your own:

_____

_____

_____

_____

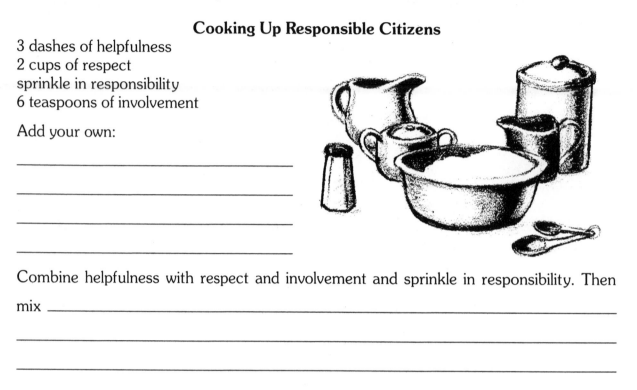

Combine helpfulness with respect and involvement and sprinkle in responsibility. Then mix _____

_____

_____

_____

42

GA1327

Bull's-eye

From the following list circle five attitudes or actions that you believe in strongly, as a citizen.

a. I believe it is important to give to the poor.
b. I believe it is important to conserve water and electricity.
c. I believe it is important to help others.
d. I believe it is important to get involved in meetings and organizations to help make changes when necessary.
e. I believe it is important to be respectful and kind to those around me.
f. I believe it is important to help save the environment in whatever way I can.
g. I believe it is important to care for the sick in some way.
h. I believe it is important to care for the elderly in some way.

Write the letter of each of your five choices in the circles below, putting the belief you value the most in the highest numbered circle and so on. On the scorecard below, give yourself the indicated number of points every time you act on one of your beliefs. For example, if you value most giving to the poor, every time you give to the poor give yourself 150 points. See how many points you can get at the end of a week.

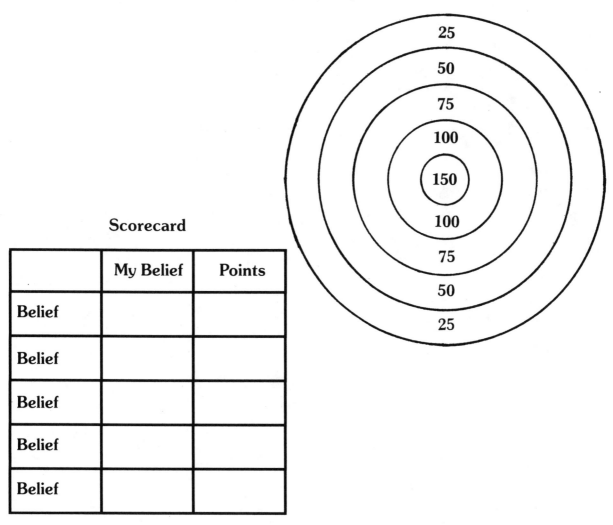

Scorecard

	My Belief	Points
Belief		
Belief		
Belief		
Belief		
Belief		

GA1327

Chapter 3

What Is Responsible Citizenship?

"The first requisite of a good citizen in this republic of ours is that he shall be able and willing to pull his weight."

Theodore Roosevelt, 1902

GA1327

Introduction

In this chapter you will learn to distinguish responsible citizenship from poor citizenship. In the activity What's Wrong with This Picture, you will compare what four people say about responsible citizenship to what they actually do. You will decide for yourself how much commitment is necessary to be a responsible citizen.

Once you have completed this activity, you will be ready to tackle some more subtle problems. Responsible citizenship dilemmas present situations where responsible citizens with good intentions may disagree about the best course of action. Then in Which Americans Do You Agree With, you will confront a fundamental symbolic issue, the sanctity of the American flag.

The next part of Chapter 3 challenges you to determine for yourself how you must act in order to be a responsible citizen. The exercises help you to develop standards for your own behavior. By the end of the chapter, you will have a chance to describe what responsible citizenship means to you and to conduct a search for the ideal citizen.

45

GA1327

Word Play

Begin by writing these words' definitions in the boxes below. Use your own dictionary. Each of these words is hidden in the activities of Chapter 3. When you discover one of the words while working on an activity, put an *X* in that word's box and write the page number you found it on. (You may find a word more than once and on many pages. Write each of the pages you find it on.) See if you can get BINGO by putting an *X* in every box. Good luck!

B	I	N	G	O
industrialized Page # _____ Definition _____ _____ _____	borne Page # _____ Definition _____ _____ _____	morals Page # _____ Definition _____ _____ _____	optimist Page # _____ Definition _____ _____ _____	perpetual Page # _____ Definition _____ _____ _____
habitat Page # _____ Definition _____ _____ _____	rampage Page # _____ Definition _____ _____ _____	tolerate Page # _____ Definition _____ _____ _____	responsible Page # _____ Definition _____ _____ _____	inherent Page # _____ Definition _____ _____ _____
renewable Page # _____ Definition _____ _____ _____	sacrifice Page # _____ Definition _____ _____ _____	FREE	environment Page # _____ Definition _____ _____ _____	resources Page # _____ Definition _____ _____ _____
veto Page # _____ Definition _____ _____ _____	traits Page # _____ Definition _____ _____ _____	accelerate Page # _____ Definition _____ _____ _____	desertification Page # _____ Definition _____ _____ _____	vigilante Page # _____ Definition _____ _____ _____
convictions Page # _____ Definition _____ _____ _____	persuasive Page # _____ Definition _____ _____ _____	authorities Page # _____ Definition _____ _____ _____	truncheon Page # _____ Definition _____ _____ _____	desecration Page # _____ Definition _____ _____ _____

GA1327

Responsible Citizenship Dilemmas

Read the following dilemmas. Think through the issues and decide what a responsible citizen would do. Then discuss your answers with your classmates and teacher.

1. Jan lives next door to Mary. Jan has not liked Mary for years. Jan feels Mary does not help keep the neighborhood clean. She does not clean up after her dog. She litters the streets and never puts the trash out for the garbage truck on the right days. She never participates in the community meetings. She has loud parties, and she lets her dog bark and howl all through the night. Mary even leaves garden tools and raked leaves on Jan's property.

   Given the facts above, do you think Jan would be a responsible citizen if she were to:

   - gossip about Mary to her neighbors?
   - report her to health authorities?
   - leave her trash on Mary's property?
   - not speak to her when she sees her outside?
   - invite and encourage her to attend community meetings?
   - speak to Mary about her concerns?

   Based on your answers, decide which of the statements below most closely represents your views.

   - A responsible citizen does not need to concern himself with difficult neighbors.
   - A responsible citizen is someone who treats his neighbors with respect even if he/she does not like him/her.
   - A responsible citizen treats his neighbor the same way the neighbor is treating him.

2. A war has broken out between Bill's country and a bordering nation. Bill disagrees with the reasons for the war and believes that fighting will not solve the difficulties between the countries. He also knows it will cost many lives and much property.

   Given the facts above, do you think Bill is a responsible citizen if he:

   - serves in the army because it is his duty?
   - does not serve in the army because the war goes against his values and beliefs?

   Based on your answers, circle one of the statements below.

   - A responsible citizen serves his country no matter what his personal values, beliefs, and convictions are.
   - A responsible citizen always stands behind his values and morals.

47

GA1327

3. Mrs. Jones is speaking out at the community meeting. She is angry over the town plans to build large hotels in the neighborhood. She is campaigning to veto this decision. Most other people at the meeting are in favor of the hotel construction and believe it will raise property values. Every time Mrs. Jones speaks, the rest of the group asks her to sit down and be quiet because she is taking up valuable time. They remind her that she will not get her way.

Given the facts above, do you think responsible citizens:
- let others speak even if they don't like what they are hearing?
- give community members the right to protest and disagree with issues?
- should try to get each other to think and live the same way?

Based on your answers, circle a statement below.
- A responsible citizen tolerates differences and listens to all points of views.
- A responsible citizen tries to protect himself and others by not tolerating differences between people and trying to get everyone to be alike.

4. Martha finally saved enough allowance to be able to go to the basketball game. She gave up many things to go to this big event and is very excited. It means a lot to her to cheer on her school team and be with her friends. As she is walking home from school awaiting tomorrow's big event, a woman with a young child approaches her begging for money. The woman explains to Martha that her young child is very sick and hungry and she is desperate for some money to save the child. Martha knows if she gives her any of her change she will not be able to go to the game.

Given the facts above, do you think Martha would be a responsible citizen if she were to:
- sacrifice what she has for someone less fortunate?
- take care of herself and her own desires?
- not give the woman money since she herself had so little, but instead finds someone to take care of the mother and child?
- ignore beggars?

Based on your answers, circle one of the statements below.
- A responsible citizen sacrifices for the needs of others.
- A responsible citizen always takes care of himself first.
- A responsible citizen finds a way to help those in need.

To be a responsible citizen, I must remember _____

_____

_____

_____

_____

_____

What's Wrong with This Picture?

Look at each picture. Under each illustration describe how the characters are not behaving like responsible citizens although talking to each other about responsible citizenship values.

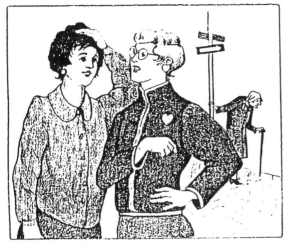

Picture 1

Picture 2

Picture 3

Picture 4

Discuss what is happening in each picture with your teacher and classmates. Try to answer this question:

> In order to be a responsible citizen, does a person have to demonstrate his attitudes, or is it enough just to talk about them? Explain.

To be a responsible citizen, I must remember _____

_____

_____

_____

_____

GA1327

Responsible Citizenship in Action

Read this excerpt from a newspaper article and answer the questions below.

- Mr. Kay, a young man in his late 20's walking to his neighborhood grocery, becomes witness to a mugging. He sees two men grab a woman's purse and run up the street he is walking down. Mr. Kay chases after them, grabs and holds them, gets the woman's purse back, ties their hands behind their backs, and brings them to the police.

1. What is the action or attitude described that exhibits responsible citizenship?

   _____

   _____

2. Do you think Mr. Kay should have taken the law into his own hands or instead called the police to catch the muggers? Explain your reason.

   _____

   _____

   In the back of the book, find the definition of *vigilante*. _____

   _____

3. What are the rewards for this man? What are the risks? _____

   _____

4. In which of the circumstances listed below could you see yourself doing this act of citizenship?

   Only if I . . .

   were forced ☐

   were to receive a big reward ☐

   knew for sure I would not get hurt ☐

   would do this no matter what ☐

5. What set of values are demonstrated by this citizen's actions?

   _____

6. What values do you have that help you to be a responsible citizen? What values do you need to develop? Examples are honesty and respect for others. _____

   _____

To be a responsible citizen, I must remember _____

_____

_____

GA1327

Everyday Citizenship

See how many ways you can think of to be a responsible citizen in a grocery store. Make this activity a contest between you and your classmates. See who can think of the most ways in the shortest amount of time. On your mark, get set, go. You have four minutes.

For example: Don't leave a grocery cart blocking an aisle.

_____

_____

_____

_____

_____

_____

_____

_____

_____

Think of the many ways to be a responsible citizen in other situations and places such as your classroom, school bus, backyard. On your mark, get set, go!

Discuss with your teacher and classmates the answers to the following questions:

What laws, if any, are necessary in grocery stores, classrooms, school buses? Why or why not? Do you think citizens are obedient without laws in these places? Why or why not?

To be a responsible citizen, I must remember _____

_____

_____

_____

_____

GA1327

Which Americans Do You Agree With?

Some people in the United States debate whether or not damaging, burning, or trampling on the country's flag should be legal or illegal. Read the paragraph under each flag and decide what you believe about flag burning. Color the flag above the paragraph which comes closest to describing your view about it. Circle the letter of the paragraph you agree with.

Then those classmates who agree with paragraph A should stand on one side of the classroom while those students who agree with paragraph B should stand on the opposite side of the room. Each side should discuss their views and debate the issues. Be prepared to tell the class whether your choice of paragraph is based on what makes the most sense to you or on which paragraph your friends chose.

A. Some patriotic Americans want to make desecration of the U.S. flag a crime. They believe the flag is sacred. Purposefully damaging the U.S. flag, they believe, would demonstrate opposition to American values and to democracy. They believe that to oppose flag desecration is to support the American values the flag represents. This group of citizens has proposed an amendment to the United States Constitution which would say "The Congress and the states shall have power to prohibit the physical desecration of the flag of the United States."

B. Other patriotic Americans oppose making desecration of the flag illegal. They say that flag desecration is a form of free speech. They believe that all Americans should oppose any attempt to restrict free speech, even if they personally oppose what someone has to say. They also warn that making flag desecration illegal would require a change to the Bill of Rights. They warn that the costs of government intrusion into people's individual behavior far outweigh any distaste for flag burning.

GA1327

Flag Burning

Consider the following quotations about flag burning. Discuss each quotation with your teacher and classmates. Decide whether you would support or oppose a constitutional amendment. Find out how to make your views known to your elected representatives.

- "This is the time when true lovers of the flag and what it symbolizes need to stand up for it . . . . We don't want to desecrate our Bill of Rights in order to permit the prosecution of a handful of peaceful protestors." American Bar Association

- "[Desecration of the flag] is malicious conduct and we ought to have a right to contain it." Senator Robert Dole

- "Punishing desecration of the flag dilutes the very freedom that makes this emblem so revered, and worth revering." Supreme Court Justice William Brennan

- I disapprove of what you say, but I will defend to the death your right to say it.

- People who burn the flag may be protesting not the ideals for which it stands but rather the degree to which their country has fallen short of those ideals.

- Rather than dwell on burning flags, let us examine the causes of flag burning.

- ". . . A truncheon is a very effective tool for a community trying to teach its members which opinions are acceptable." From a letter to *The Wall Street Journal**

- "Free speech . . . means the right not to agree with the community; the right not to accept what its symbols have come to represent . . . ." From the same letter*

- A community has rights superior to an individual's. Community standards are established to provide a stable foundation in our society.

*Reprinted with permission of *The Wall Street Journal*, copyright 1990, Dow Jones and Company, Inc. All rights reserved.

GA1327

What Can You Do to Help?

Be a responsible citizen by getting involved, organizing citizen groups, and brainstorming ways to help save the environment. Read about the state of the world's environment. Choose a category that you are particularly interested in and join together with other classmates also interested in this area of the environment. Together brainstorm what you, as citizens, can do to protect this aspect of the environment. Make a long list. Discuss with your teacher and classmates your ideas and begin the projects needed to help care for and save the environment. Plan to meet weekly with your group.

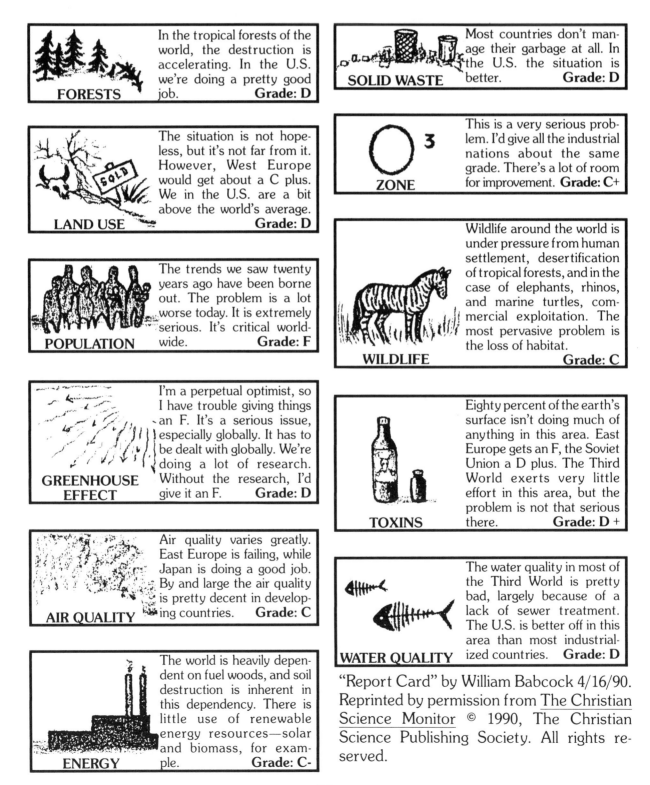

FORESTS — In the tropical forests of the world, the destruction is accelerating. In the U.S. we're doing a pretty good job. **Grade: D**

LAND USE — The situation is not hopeless, but it's not far from it. However, West Europe would get about a C plus. We in the U.S. are a bit above the world's average. **Grade: D**

POPULATION — The trends we saw twenty years ago have been borne out. The problem is a lot worse today. It is extremely serious. It's critical worldwide. **Grade: F**

GREENHOUSE EFFECT — I'm a perpetual optimist, so I have trouble giving things an F. It's a serious issue, especially globally. It has to be dealt with globally. We're doing a lot of research. Without the research, I'd give it an F. **Grade: D**

AIR QUALITY — Air quality varies greatly. East Europe is failing, while Japan is doing a good job. By and large the air quality is pretty decent in developing countries. **Grade: C**

ENERGY — The world is heavily dependent on fuel woods, and soil destruction is inherent in this dependency. There is little use of renewable energy resources—solar and biomass, for example. **Grade: C-**

SOLID WASTE — Most countries don't manage their garbage at all. In the U.S. the situation is better. **Grade: D**

ZONE — This is a very serious problem. I'd give all the industrial nations about the same grade. There's a lot of room for improvement. **Grade: C+**

WILDLIFE — Wildlife around the world is under pressure from human settlement, desertification of tropical forests, and in the case of elephants, rhinos, and marine turtles, commercial exploitation. The most pervasive problem is the loss of habitat. **Grade: C**

TOXINS — Eighty percent of the earth's surface isn't doing much of anything in this area. East Europe gets an F, the Soviet Union a D plus. The Third World exerts very little effort in this area, but the problem is not that serious there. **Grade: D +**

WATER QUALITY — The water quality in most of the Third World is pretty bad, largely because of a lack of sewer treatment. The U.S. is better off in this area than most industrialized countries. **Grade: D**

"Report Card" by William Babcock 4/16/90. Reprinted by permission from The Christian Science Monitor © 1990, The Christian Science Publishing Society. All rights reserved.

GA1327

What Can I Do to Help?

The category I have chosen to get involved with is _____.

I am particularly interested and concerned about this aspect of the environment because

_____

_____.

Some of the ideas I have to help save and care for this aspect of the environment include

_____

_____

_____

_____

_____

_____

_____

_____

Laws that are necessary to help protect our environment include _____

_____

_____

Ways in which I would like to get these laws passed include _____

_____

The project (I/my group) decided to work on is _____.

(My/Our) hope, through this project, is to _____

_____

Projects can include petitions, writing letters, educating the public, creating ideas for inventions or organizing citizen groups, banning items, etc.

To be a responsible citizen, I must remember _____

_____

_____

_____

_____

GA1327

Wanted

Imagine the type of citizen you would want to be a part of your community. How would the person act? What would the person look like?

Design a WANTED poster of the ideal citizen. Follow the directions below.

Cut and paste a picture or photo in the box below of the citizen you are WANTING. It can be a picture or photo of someone you know, it can be a picture of someone you cut from a magazine, or if you want, you can draw a picture of a real or pretend person.

Description:
In the box below, describe the person physically and also describe his/her personality traits. Example: Wanted—person with good humor, a concern for others and ability to get along with others.

Fill in the blanks.

This person was last seen *in* _____.

He/She was _____

_____,

once again showing himself/herself to be an active and responsible citizen.

If you have seen or have any information about this person, please contact _____

_____

This person is an ideal citizen because _____

_____

Hang your WANTED poster on the bulletin board with your classmates'.

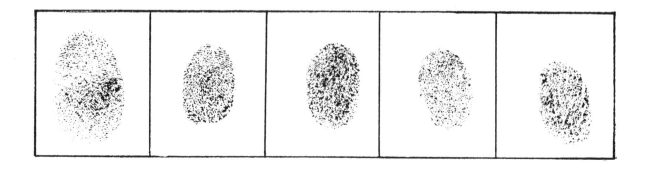

GA1327

Responsible Citizenship Winners

Explain what responsible citizenship is in your own words. Then write your name under the figure in the middle and write the names of four of your friends, classmates, teachers, or relatives under each of the other figures. Under each person's name write at least three ways these people are responsible citizens. Remember to tell each of them what you have written.

Responsible citizenship is _____

_____

Example:

Myra

1. helpful
2. always there
   if a person
   is in need
3. generous

_____	_____	_____	_____	_____
1. ____	1. ____	1. ____	1. ____	1. ____
2. ____	2. ____	2. ____	2. ____	2. ____
3. ____	3. ____	3. ____	3. ____	3. ____

The personality traits responsible citizens have include _____

_____

Write Your Own Story

Write a story. Include each of the following words somewhere in the story. Use the glossary in the back of your book to find the meaning of each word.

citizen	civil	civil defense	civil war
citizenship	civilian	civil liberty	civil service
civic	civilize	civil rights	

Read your story to your classmates. Make a booklet of your citizenship stories.

GA1327

Chapter 4

What Is Communicating in Communities All About?

"No one can make you feel inferior without your consent."

Eleanor Roosevelt

Introduction

The community is made up of many individual citizens and groups of citizens. These individuals and groups naturally have competing and conflicting goals and interests.

The strength of the community depends greatly on the ability of these individuals and groups to communicate. Through effective communication, individuals and groups can uncover ways to best meet their own needs without harming the interests of other groups.

This chapter helps you to build your own communication skills. As you improve your ability to communicate, you will discover many opportunities to enrich your own life, and to appreciate your differences from other members of the community. Strong communication skills will help you, your family, and your friends be good citizens and lead better lives.

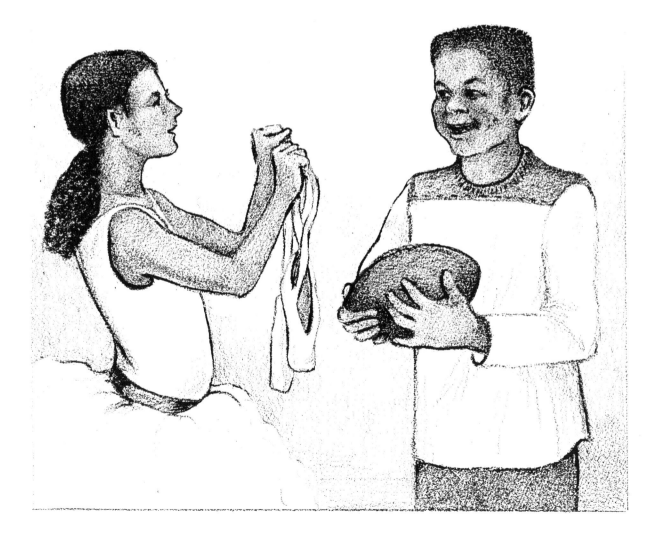

GA1327

Word Play

Use the context clues to help you guess the meanings of the following words. Then look each up in your own dictionary and write its meaning below.

1. If you compliment her, her *self-esteem* will improve.

   Guess _____

   Definition _____

2. She has the least skills of anyone on her team so she feels *inferior*.

   Guess _____

   Definition _____

3. His *submissive* personality causes him never to state his own opinions.

   Guess _____

   Definition _____

4. Mary's father did not like other ethnic groups and would often make *slurs* about them.

   Guess _____

   Definition _____

5. Greg liked to be *dominant* in a group so that others would look up to him. This made him feel *superior*.

   Guess (dominant) _____

   Guess (superior) _____

   Definition (dominant) _____

   Definition (superior) _____

6. Jane's poor *communication* skills caused her friend Kathy to feel *resentment* toward her since she never knew what she was trying to say.

   Guess (communication) _____

   Guess (resentment) _____

   Definition (communication) _____

   Definition (resentment) _____

7. *Justice* is served when citizens obey laws, and those who don't pay the consequences.

   Guess _____

   Definition _____

Seesaw Communication

Read the following dialogue between Mike and Sam. As you read it, see how it affects your feelings.

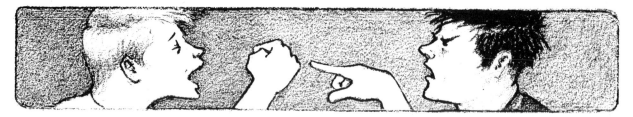

Mike: You're such a loser. You can't do anything right, ever!

Sam: Look who is talking. You can't even get a ball over the net when we play volleyball.

Mike: Oh! As if you are so great. You go home crying to Mommy every time you get a little cut or scrape. You are a real wimp.

Sam: You are the wimp. You are so skinny and scared of your own shadow. Don't call me the wimp.

Mike: You are the wimp. None of the kids like you.

Sam: I know Joe, Art, Don hate you. They think you are weird.

Mike: As if I care if those kids like me. They don't rate in my book.

Answer the following questions:

Notice that Mike and Sam speak to each other as if they are on a seesaw. Mike says mean things in order to put down Sam and then Sam feels put down. So what does Sam have to do to make himself feel big again? _____

_____

Now Mike feels put down and small. What does he do to make himself feel powerful and on top of things? _____

_____

Each tries to prove the other wrong so he is right. Have you ever done this? Do you think this is an effective way to communicate? Why or why not? _____

_____

Do you think problems can get solved this way? Why or why not? _____

_____

How do you think they feel about themselves after communicating like this? _____

_____

What is each trying to prove to the other? To himself? _____

_____

Have you ever felt like Mike or Sam? _____

Did you ever try to feel better about yourself by putting the other person down? _____

Did it really help? Why or why not? _____

What do you think is a more effective way to communicate and solve problems? _____

_____

What do you think is a more effective way to feel good about yourself and others? _____

_____

Seesaw Madness

Let's take a closer look at Mike and Sam's seesaw communication. The person trying to push up on the seesaw is possibly trying to feel superior, dominate, in control, right, and powerful while trying to make the person going down on the seesaw feel inferior, submissive, wrong, and powerless. The way this is being accomplished is through put-downs, slurs, sometimes abuse, and violence. Find three examples in your school, community, or the news of situations where a seesaw cycle of communication between people or groups exists. Summarize each situation below.

Example:
Women fighting for equal rights with men—they are fighting by putting men down, calling them names.

Racial issues—a gang of white boys attacks and kills a black boy. Black community verbally attacks whites.

Discuss with your teacher and classmates how the individuals or groups involved in each situation could communicate more effectively.

                                      GA1327

Seesaw Slurs

In seesaw communication people or groups of people rarely solve their problems because they do not know what problems they are actually trying to solve. Their real purpose in their struggle is to put the other persons or groups down in order to make themselves look and feel right, powerful, and in control.

Choose a topic below. Write the two conflicting sides of the issue on either side of the seesaw. Write all the slurs and put-downs you can think of that the higher side of the seesaw will say about the lower in order to try to stay dominant.

Seesaw 1: Racial Issues—Blacks Against Whites

For example:
Whites are all
uptight.

Seesaw 2: Sexist Issues—Males Against Females

For example:
Females are the
weaker sex.

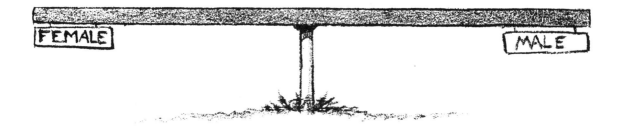

GA1327

Being Right or Finding a Solution

Read the following dialogues and see if you can notice the differences in the communication styles.

Being Right

Mike: You're such a loser. You can't do anything right, ever!

Sam: Look who is talking. You can't even get a ball over the net when we play volleyball.

Mike: Oh! As if you are so great. You go home crying to Mommy every time you get a little cut or scrape. You are a real wimp.

Sam: You are the wimp. You are so skinny and scared of your own shadow. Don't call me the wimp.

Mike: You are the wimp. None of the kids like you.

Sam: I know Joe, Art, Don hate you. They think you are weird.

Mike: As if I care if those kids like me. They don't rate in my book.

Finding a Solution

Sue: I can never fall asleep because you always keep the radio blaring.

Shari: I didn't know it kept you awake.

Sue: It does and then I can't concentrate in school the next day.

Shari: Well I can't fall asleep without music.

Sue: And I can't fall asleep with music, and we are stuck sharing the same room. What are we going to do?

Shari: Let's try to think of what we can do so we don't keep getting mad at each other.

Sue: You could listen to music in the living room until you get real tired, and then you could come in and go to sleep.

Shari: No, that won't work for me because I would just get drowsy and fall asleep on the couch. Maybe you could come in to go to sleep after I'm already sleeping.

Sue: No, then I can't go to bed or be in my room when I want. I have an idea! Maybe you could wear headphones to sleep.

Shari: Yeah! That's an idea. Maybe Mom and Dad would buy me headphones—a Walkman— I've always wanted them and that might solve our problem!

Answer the following questions and then discuss your answers with your teacher and classmates.

1. What are Sue's and Shari's conflicting needs? What do they need to find a solution to?

_____

What are Mike's and Sam's conflicting needs? What do they need to find a solution to? Do we know? Do they know? _____

2. Once Sue and Shari understand their different needs, how do they go about finding a solution?

_____

Do they put each other down in the process? _____

Does either of them try to make herself look better than the other? _____

Do they condemn each other's needs? Their own? Do they give up their own needs?

_____

Does it seem that it is more important for Sue and Shari to find a solution to their problem or for one of them to prove how right she is and how wrong the other person is?

_____

How would you feel if you were Sue or Shari? _____

Have you ever worked out your differences with someone like Sue and Shari did? _____

How did you feel about yourself and the other person? _____

How did you feel about the solution? _____

Did Sue and Shari both find a way to get what they want and still like each other and be friends? _____

GA1327

3. Once Mike and Sam understood their differences (conflict), how did they go about finding a solution? _____

Do they put each other down in the process? _____ Does that solve anything? _____

Does either of them try to make himself look better than the other? _____ Does

that solve anything? _____

What is Mike trying to prove? _____

What is Sam trying to prove? _____

Does it seem that it is more important for Mike and Sam to find a solution to their conflict or for them to prove how right one is and how wrong the other person is?

_____

How would you feel if you were Mike or Sam? How might they feel about themselves?

Each other? Their solution or lack of a solution? _____

Have you ever worked out your differences with someone like Mike and Sam? _____

How did you feel about yourself? The other person? _____

Did you come to a solution or just a more intense battle? _____

What will one person need to do in order to stop the battle from intensifying?

_____

Can Mike and Sam both find a way to get what they want and still like each other

and remain friends? Why or why not? _____

Think of a conflict you have with someone in your life right now. Decide if you want to find a solution to your conflict so that you can both try to get what you want and live in peace with each other. Decide if what you really want is to prove how right you are and how wrong the other person is. If you really want to find the solution, write down as many solutions as you can think of to resolve the problem. Ask the other person to do the same. Then find a time to read them to each other and decide which could possibly work for both of you and which could not. Cross out the ones that could not work. Try to find a solution that will work for both of you. Be creative!

Possible Solutions

If what you really want is to prove how right you are and how wrong the other person is, acknowledge this to each other. Don't pretend to be wanting to solve a problem when all you really want to do is prove how great you are. Now list all the ways you are going to prove how right, great, important, powerful, superior, and dominant you are.

All the ways I try to prove that I'm better than everyone else are _____

_____

_____

GA1327

Taking a Closer Look

Let's take a closer look at the communication between Sue and Shari. Sue and Shari have conflicting needs. One person needs to fall asleep to music and the other person can only fall asleep if it is quiet. Neither person is right or wrong, better or worse. They simply have differences. When people live together in communities, often there are many conflicting needs because of people's differences. Sue and Shari respected each other's differences and their own. Neither person tried to condemn the other person for being different or condemn herself. They were willing to acknowledge the difference and try to find a workable solution in order to be able to live together.

As citizens, we live together in our communities. We must be able to find ways to live together with our differences. This often takes problem solving. Find three examples in your school, community, or in the news of situations that have been resolved or are being resolved with the communication style of Sue and Shari. Summarize the situations below. Discuss with your teacher and classmates.

Example:

Landlord vs. Tenants.
Tenants want more security in their apartment building. Landlord listens to their concerns and hires new doorman and hires a patrol watch. Each tenant pays an extra $10.00 per month in rent for this service. Both parties (landlord and tenants) feel satisfied and heard.

GA1327

Ignoring Needs

Read the following dialogues and see if you notice the differences in the communication.

Sue: I can never fall asleep because you always keep the radio blaring.

Shari: I didn't know it kept you awake.

Sue: It does and then I can't concentrate in school the next day.

Shari: Well I can't fall asleep without music.

Sue: And I can't fall asleep with music, and we are stuck sharing the same room. What are we going to do?

Shari: Let's try to think of what we can do so we don't keep getting mad at each other.

Sue: You could listen to music in the living room until you get real tired, and then you could come in and go to sleep.

Shari: No, that won't work for me because I would just get drowsy and fall asleep on the couch. Maybe you could come in to go to sleep after I'm already sleeping.

Sue: No, then I can't go to bed or be in my room when I want. I have an idea! Maybe you could wear headphones to sleep.

Shari: Yeah! That's an idea. Maybe Mom and Dad would buy me headphones—a Walkman—I've always wanted them and that might solve our problem!

Anne: I can never fall asleep because you always keep the radio blaring.

Debbie: I didn't know it kept you awake.

Anne: It does and then I can't concentrate in school the next day.

Debbie: Sorry but I can't fall asleep without music.

Anne: OK. I'll just try to get used to it or just do the best I can in school the next day. I hope you are not angry with me for telling you that I had problems with your music.

Debbie: No. That's okay.

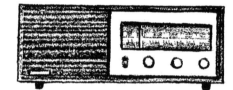

Answer the following questions and then discuss your answers with your teacher and classmates.

1. What is the difference between Sue and Shari's dialogue and Anne and Debbie's?

_____

2. In which dialogue do both people get what they want or need? _____

In which dialogue does one person give up what she needs so that the other person won't be angry? _____

3. Have you ever given up trying to get what you want or need or not even asked for it so that someone else would not be angry or upset? Explain. _____

_____

4. Which style of communicating leads to better problem solving? Why? _____

_____

5. Why do you think Anne easily gave up going after what she wanted? _____

6. What would you have done if you were Debbie? Would you have let the dialogue stop there? Why or why not? _____

GA1327

Avoiding Trouble

Let's take a closer look at the communication between Anne and Debbie. Problems are best resolved when everyone involved feels listened to and feels as if his needs are considered. Although it was Anne who backed down and gave up rather quickly trying to get her need for quiet met, she will probably feel resentful of Debbie every night when she tries to get some sleep, and she will feel angrier and angrier. Since Anne seems afraid to directly go after what she needs, she will either forget her own needs and do without or she will indirectly try to get back at Debbie possibly through seesaw communication. She'll ignore Debbie or act snappy, or argue and complain about other things, or she'll try to put Debbie down somehow. So, although it looks like their communication was smooth and complete, actually nothing was resolved, and they have positioned themselves for more battles.

The same kind of poor communication and problem solving takes place in communities. Sometimes people or groups ignore their needs and therefore ignore fighting for their rights, social change, and justice. Yet, resentment between people and groups builds. Find three cases in your school, community, or in the news of situations that are examples. Summarize below and discuss with your teacher and classmates.

Example:

Tenants in the apartment building tried to ignore that the walls in the hallways were chipping and the building was not being maintained. Most tenants ignored this because they felt they could not do anything to change the situation. Finally, when the building began to deteriorate, angry tenants stormed the landlord's office demanding changes or threatening to move out.

Rewrite the Script

Rewrite the Mike and Sam dialogue so that both of them end up feeling good about themselves and each other and so that problems get solved.

Mike: _____

Sam: _____

Mike: _____

Sam: _____

Mike: _____

Sam: _____

Mike: _____

Sam: _____

Mike: _____

Sam: _____

Mike: _____

Sam: _____

Mike: _____

Sam: _____

Mike: _____

Sam: _____

Discuss with your teacher and classmates why your revised dialogue leads to better communication and problem solving and improved self-esteem than the seesaw communication.

70

GA1327

Chapter 5

What Do You Think of These Citizens?

"It is not always the same thing to be a good person and a good citizen."

Aristotle, 4th century B.C.

Introduction

In this book we have examined what is citizenship, what is responsible citizenship, the values and attitudes which contribute to responsible citizenship, and the great importance of communication skills in dealing with community issues. Now you have an opportunity to focus on what you have discovered and practiced. In this chapter, you will be able to evaluate the citizenship qualities of a very wide range of people. These people have been selected not because of how well-known they are, but rather because their biographies demonstrate a very wide range of issues each of us is exposed to as a citizen. The knowledge you gain from this chapter and the evaluation skills you develop here will help you to live fuller lives and to grapple with the difficult issues which your society will face.

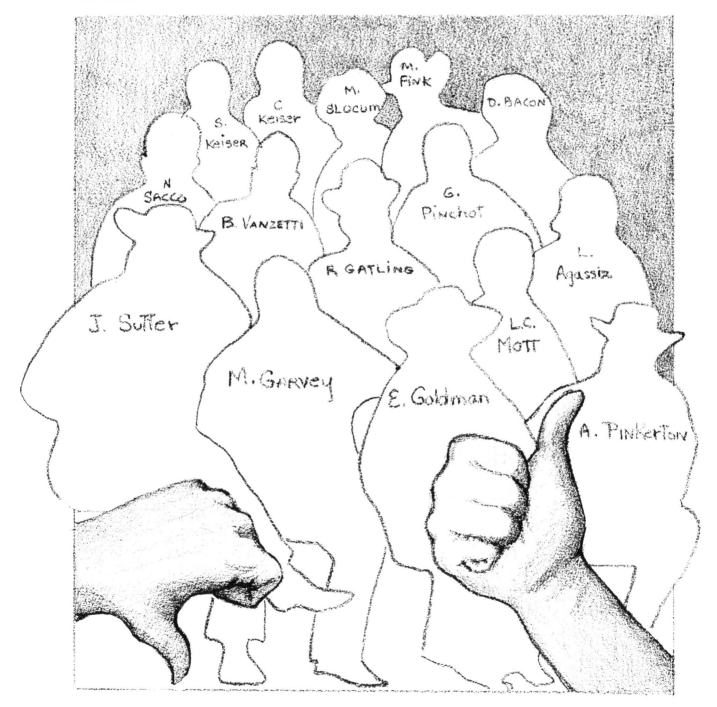

GA1327

Word Play

Find each of these vocabulary words in this chapter. Underline the word with a blue crayon on the page you find it and circle it with an orange crayon on its page when you have found and written its definition below. Use your own dictionary. Complete the vocabulary before you do each exercise.

Mike Fink
frontiersman _____
marksman _____
keelboatman _____
reputation _____
legendary _____

Richard Gatling
sowing _____
plow _____
propeller _____
patented _____

John Sutter
bankruptcy _____
prosperous _____
prospectors _____

Marcus Garvey
descent _____
scholar _____
rousing _____
prestige _____
ventures _____
fraud _____
deported _____
wane _____
obscure _____
impoverished _____

Keiser
penetrate _____
reared _____

Louis Agassiz
monumental _____
fossilized _____
geological _____
naturalized _____

Emma Goldman
migrated _____
inciting _____
suppressed _____
subversive _____
hysteria _____
alien _____

GA1327

Margaret Slocum	estate	
	philanthropy	
	financier	

Gifford Pinchot	conservationists	
	commission	
	controversy	
	reforms	

Lucretia Mott	fervor	
	abolition	
	opposition	
	revoke	
	status	

Sacco Vanzetti	draft	
	socialism	
	philosophical	
	anarchist	
	prejudice	
	revolution	
	circumstantial	
	appealed	

Allan Pinkerton	anthracite	
	cooper	
	counterfeiters	
	"way station"	
	assassinate	
	inaugurated	
	counterespionage	
	fraud	
	labor movements	
	strikebreaker	

Delia Bacon	obsessed	
	obscure	
	verge	
	abandoned	
	ridiculed	

GA1327

Mike Fink

Before the American Civil War, Fink was well-known as a frontiersman and a folk hero. He was born at Fort Pitt, the site of the modern city of Pittsburgh, about 1770. He was widely known as a marksman and a scout. Apparently Davy Crockett was even impressed by Mike Fink's skill with a rifle.

After fighting Native American Indians in western Pennsylvania, Mike Fink worked as a keelboatman on the boats that traveled the Ohio and Mississippi Rivers. Keelboatmen were known to be combative and loud, and he was known as the "king of the keelboatmen." Fink was an able storyteller and used his imagination to build his reputation as "half horse, half alligator."

As the keelboat trade was replaced by steamboats, Mike Fink joined a fur trapping expedition and traveled to the Rocky Mountains. There he died a violent death, the cause of which cannot be determined, since so many stories about his reputed prowess circulated among the population. As a public figure, he grew to become legendary after his death. He lost popularity after the Civil War.

Mike Fink Activities

Discussion Questions

Discuss with your teacher and classmates the following questions:

1. Why do you think Mike Fink was so well-known before the war?

2. What makes Mike Fink a responsible citizen?

3. How did he contribute to his community? Was he a burden in anyway? If so, how?

Imagine and Illustrate

Using your imagination, make up a story about the end of Mike Fink's life. How did he die? Why? Where? Also explain why his popularity declined after the Civil War. Draw pictures to go along with your story. Share your stories and pictures with your teacher and classmates.

Make Believe

Make believe you were a keelboatman and a marksman and rode on the boats that traveled the Ohio and Mississippi Rivers just like Fink. Make up an adventure that happens on your journey and role-play it with your classmates. What do you imagine your life to be like? What might be important to you in the future that is not important to you now? How would you be contributing to your community as a keelboatman and marksman? Would you have liked knowing Mike Fink? Why or why not?

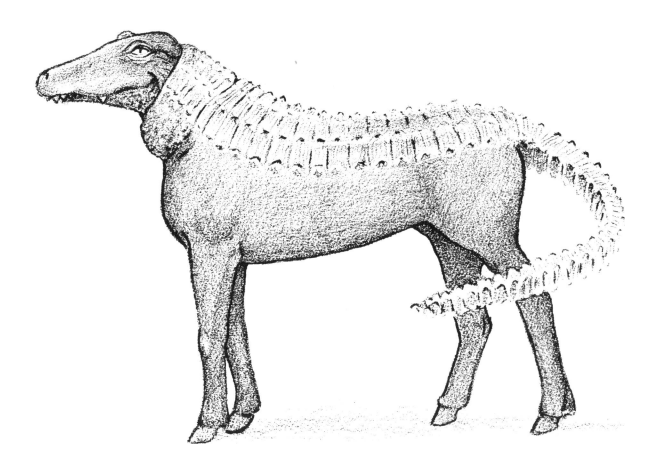

GA1327

Richard Gatling

Richard Gatling had a great deal of mechanical ability and imagination. As a child in North Carolina in the 1820's, he helped his father develop new machines for sowing and thinning cotton. He became a schoolteacher, then a store manager. He invented a screw propeller for ships. In 1844 Gatling moved to St. Louis, where he ran a business making his cotton sowing machine.

In St. Louis, Richard Gatling continued to explore new interests and to invent new things. After contracting smallpox, Gatling decided to train as a medical doctor. He finished in 1850. He invented a machine to break hemp (a plant fiber used in making ropes, etc.) and a steam-powered plow. Then the American Civil War broke out in 1861.

When the war started, Gatling turned his attention to designing military equipment. In 1862 he patented the first rapid-fire (or "machine") gun. The gun had ten barrels, automatic ammunition handling, and could fire 350 shots per minute. It used the newly developed brass cartridge casings, which were stronger and more reliable than earlier types. The gun was not adopted by the U.S. Army officially until 1866, so the Gatling gun was not used much during the Civil War. Eventually, Gatling improved the gun to 1200 shots per minute.

Richard Gatling Activities

Discussion Questions

Discuss with your teacher and classmates the following questions:

1. What made Richard Gatling a responsible citizen?

2. In what ways did Richard Gatling contribute to the society around him? Was he a burden in some way?

3. What responsibility does an inventor bear, if any, for how his or her inventions are put to use?

Imagine and Invent

Would you like to be an inventor? What would you like to invent? Think about the society in which you live right now. What invention would help make citizens' lives more comfortable? Safer? More time effective?

Get together with your classmates and discuss your ideas. Brainstorm with each other and begin creating and inventing!

GATLING GUN

GA1327

John Sutter

John Sutter was a pioneer in California. He was born in 1803 in the Grand Duchy of Baden, which is currently part of Germany. Sutter grew up there and in Switzerland. Since his parents were from Switzerland, Sutter was considered to be a Swiss citizen. Consequently, he had to serve in the Swiss Army.

Sutter had dreamed of traveling to the western part of North America since he was a child. Eventually he fled from Switzerland to avoid a bankruptcy lawsuit, leaving his wife and family behind. He sailed to America by boat from France and settled in Missouri, where he became a trader. Two years later he fled again to avoid paying the bills he owed.

This time he traveled west to Vancouver, then to Honolulu, and on to Alaska, before making his way to California in 1839. At that time California was a province of Mexico. Upon his arrival in San Francisco, Sutter visited the governor of the Province. Governor Alvarado granted Sutter 50,000 acres to start a settlement. Today Sutter's property is the site of the city of Sacramento.

During the 1840's, Sutter built up a large ranch with 4200 head of cattle, 2000 horses, and 2000 sheep. He also traded with fur trappers from the Rocky and the Sierra Nevada mountain ranges and with settlers traveling west. He was prosperous, and his family traveled from Switzerland to join him.

However, on January 24, 1848, one of Sutter's employees discovered gold on Sutter's property. The California Gold Rush followed. All Sutter's workers quit to look for gold. Prospectors stole all his animals and took over his land. He went bankrupt within three years and spent the rest of his life trying to get financial relief from the U.S. government, which had taken over control of California following the Mexican War.

GA1327

John Sutter Activities

Discussion Questions

Discuss with your teacher and classmates the following questions:

1. Was John Sutter a responsible Swiss citizen? Why or why not?

2. Was Sutter trustworthy? A responsible husband and father?

3. What did Sutter contribute to his society? Was he a burden in some way?

4. Would you try to obtain a special privilege or benefit from your government? Would this special treatment help or hinder other citizens?

5. Would you say Sutter got what he deserved? Was he treated fairly? Why or why not?

Make Believe and Create

Make believe you were part of the California Gold Rush. Find out as many facts as you can about this historical time and write a make-believe story about your personal adventure across the country with your family. What happened to you before, during and after? Role-play your story with your classmates.

Imagine and Discuss

Imagine you are living peacefully in your home and little community. Imagine suddenly hundreds and then thousands of people try to take over your home and move into your town because they have discovered the value of your home and land. Do you think the government should restrict this kind of takeover from happening by your having some rights to ownership, or do you believe it is a free society and the government does not have the right to interfere? Discuss with your teacher and classmates.

Draw

Draw a line on a world map following Sutter's route from Switzerland to France to Missouri, west to Vancouver, south to Honolulu, north to Alaska and south again to Sacramento, California.

Marcus Garvey

Marcus Garvey was an activist who fought for the rights of people of African descent. Garvey was born in Jamaica in 1887 and began working at age 14 as a printer's helper. Three years later he led the employees of a large Jamaican printing company in a strike for higher wages. Because of his involvement, no Jamaican company would employ him.

Garvey became an activist, organizing publications and political clubs. Then around 1905 Garvey moved to South America to find jobs that paid more money. By 1912 he had moved to London and was working for a scholar. Through this work he learned much about the history of Blacks.

In 1914 he returned to Jamaica, where he stayed for two years before moving to New York City. Throughout his years in Jamaica and the United States, Garvey continued to push for social reform. He established organizations, founded newspapers, organized international conferences, and gave rousing speeches. One of the organizations he founded was the Black Star Steamship Line. Garvey believed that Black-owned and operated ventures would rebuild black self-confidence and prepare Blacks for economic independence. He made plans for a "back to Africa" movement, which would settle people in Liberia.

In 1925 Garvey was found guilty of fraud in his handling of the Black Star Steamship Line's funds. He was sentenced to five years in jail. Then in 1927, President Calvin Coolidge canceled Garvey's remaining sentence. Garvey was immediately deported back to Jamaica, where he continued his work. His influence and prestige began to wane, and he moved back to London in 1935. He died there in 1940, obscure and impoverished.

GA1327

Marcus Garvey Activities

Discussion Questions

Discuss with your teacher and classmates the following questions:

1. What did Marcus Garvey contribute to his society as a citizen? Was he a burden to his society in some way?

2. How would you define an *activist*? Use your own dictionary. Why was Garvey considered one?

3. Note from the biography that Garvey moved to South America to receive higher wages. Do you think a *responsible* citizen would fight for higher wages until he won the battle rather than give up and move somewhere else where he could receive higher wages? Explain.

4. If Garvey was from Jamaica, not from the United States, then why do you suppose he wanted to fight for the rights of the people in the U.S.?

5. What did Garvey mean by *economic independence*?

6. What is a labor strike?

7. What does it mean to be *deported*? Look it up in your own dictionary. Can citizens be deported? Why or why? Write to the Immigration and Naturalization Service to find out.

8. How might people not of African descent have benefited from Garvey's work?

Imagine and Write

Imagine yourself to be an activist. What are you fighting for? What reforms do you want? How are you fighting for these changes? Write your story through an autobiography. Include your early and later life, your reforms and fights, your contributions, how you were thought about by your society, and how you died.

Charles and Sarah Keiser

The Susquehanna River (pronounced sus kwa han na) flows south through Pennsylvania from New York State to the Chesapeake Bay. Near Pennsylvania's northern border, the river forms a long, fertile valley. It is called Wyoming Valley, after the Wyoming people, who were American Indians who once lived there. The state of Wyoming was later named after this valley.

Wyoming Valley is separated from the East Coast of the United States by the Pocono Mountains and the Appalachian Mountains. For a long time the early colonial settlers who came to America were unable to penetrate these mountains. But after the Revolutionary War, settlers began to move into Wyoming Valley from the East Coast.

The early history of the valley is told in a book published in 1893, called *History of Luzerne County, Pennsylvania, with Biographical Selections*. The following passage from the book describes one of the settler families.

> "Charles and Sarah Keiser were born in Hamilton Township, Northampton County. They removed to Luzerne county about 1838, locating in Hanover Township, where they lived for a number of years as good, loyal citizens who enjoyed the full confidence of their fellow men. They reared a family of nine children, six of whom are living. George W. is the eldest in the family. He was reared and educated in Hanover Township, and learned the occupation of sawyer, which business he followed for 10 years."

GA1327

Charles and Sarah Keiser Activities

Discussion Questions

Discuss with your teacher and classmates the following questions:

1. What does it mean to be a loyal citizen?

2. What does it mean to be a citizen who enjoys the "full confidence of their fellow men"?

3. Do you want the respect of your fellow classmates and your community? Why or why not? Approval? Why or why not?

Contest

Have a contest with your fellow classmates.

- You have three minutes to list all the ways that you can think of that demonstrate you are a "loyal citizen."

  On your mark, get set, go.

  The person with the longest list should read aloud.

- Now you have three minutes to list all the ways you can think of that you "enjoy the full confidence of your fellow men."

  On your mark, get set, go.

  The person with the longest list should read aloud.

- Now you have three minutes to list all the ways you can earn the respect of your fellow citizens.

  On your mark, get set, go.

  The person with the longest list reads aloud.

GA1327

Louis Agassiz

Louis Agassiz (pronounced ag a see) was born in Switzerland in 1807. He was highly educated, holding both Ph.D. and M.D. degrees from European universities. His early work was in zoology. Agassiz's first major publication focused on the fishes of Brazil.

Agassiz was a professor at the University of Neuchatel in Switzerland between 1832 and 1846. He did a monumental, five-volume study of fossilized fish. He also conducted pioneering studies of glaciers. Agassiz became the first person to recognize a period in geologic history when the earth's climate was cold and many glaciers existed. This period of geological history is now known as the Ice Age.

In 1846 Agassiz visited the United States. Two years later he became a professor of natural history at the new Lawrence Scientific School at Harvard University. He conducted many expeditions, and wrote a book about Lake Superior. In 1859 he founded Harvard's Museum of Comparative Zoology.

Louis Agassiz became a naturalized United States citizen and spent the rest of his life in America. He was known for his outstanding teaching methods and for stimulating popular interest in natural history. He came under criticism late in his career for opposing Darwin's theory of natural selection.

GA1327

Louis Agassiz Activities

Discussion Questions

Discuss the following questions with your teacher and classmates:

1. What contributions did Louis Agassiz make to society? Was he a burden in any way?

2. What did Agassiz discover about earth's climate? How did the work of Agassiz help prepare people today to address some of the global environmental problems we now face?

3. What does it mean to become a naturalized citizen? What impact, if any, did the citizenship of Agassiz (for example: the country in which he was a citizen) have on his work?

4. When is it important to defend an idea, even if you become unpopular? When is it not?

5. What was Darwin's theory of natural selection? Would you say that the development of new theories is good citizenship? If so, how? If not, why not?

Research and Create

Choose one of the topics below. Research the topic and report to your class as many facts as you can find on the topic. Make class booklets on the topics and illustrate each one.

Topics

Ice Age
Lake Superior
Fish of Brazil
Zoology
Darwin's Theory

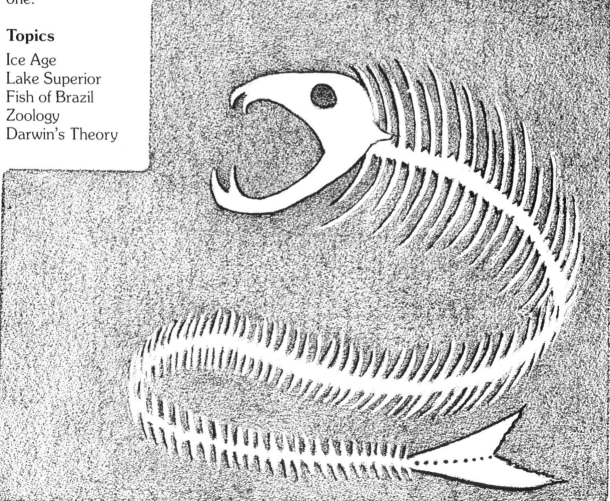

Emma Goldman

Emma Goldman was born in Lithuania and migrated to the United States in 1885, at the age of 16. She worked in clothing factories in New Haven, Connecticut, and was largely self-educated through her reading. In New Haven, she got to know people who were concerned with the rights of workers and with other social issues. In 1889 she moved to New York City.

In 1890 Goldman gave a speech to a group of unemployed workers and was put in jail for inciting a riot. When she got out, she spoke about her concerns to audiences both in the United States and in Europe. Then in 1906 she founded a magazine called *Mother Earth*. A few years later she wrote a book about her political views.

When World War I started in Europe, Goldman opposed U.S. involvement. When the U.S. did become involved, she protested against the military draft. In 1917 she was sentenced to two years in prison for her activity, and her magazine was suppressed.

By the time Emma Goldman got out of jail in 1919, the war was over. The United States was "in the throes of hysteria over a largely imaginary, subversive network of Communist elements." The government declared that Goldman was an alien and deported her and over 200 other people to the Soviet Union. She continued to lecture and to write, became involved in the Spanish Civil War in the 1930's, and lived in several Western European countries before she died in Canada in 1940.

GA1327

Emma Goldman Activities

Discussion Questions

Discuss the following questions with your teacher and classmates:

1. In reading the passage, what does it mean to be concerned with the rights of workers?

2. In the United States, one of the amendments to the Constitution guarantees the right to free speech. Find out which amendment it is. If citizens are guaranteed the right to free speech, then how could Emma Goldman have been put in jail for speaking in public?

3. What does it mean to suppress a magazine? What is censorship? Look in your glossary.

4. What is civil disobedience? Look in your glossary. Do you think Emma Goldman practiced civil disobedience? Why or why not?

5. Do you think Emma Goldman was a responsible citizen? Why or why not? What did she contribute? Was she a burden in any way? How?

6. Should a country's government have the right to suppress people who oppose the government? Why or why not?

Write and Speak Out

Write a speech on an issue that concerns you (in school, in your community, the environment, in politics or government, in your home, etc.). Take turns with your classmates standing at the podium in your classroom giving your speeches. Make sure classmates speak out on their views of the issues you presented and allow for debate and discussion. Be aware of how it feels to speak out on an issue and have people disagree with you, get angry with you, have different opinions than you, etc. Notice your response. Do you continue to stand up for what you believe, or do you withdraw or change your opinion to go along with others? Notice if you get others to understand your point of view. How do you do this?

GA1327

Margaret Slocum

Margaret Slocum was born in 1828 in Syracuse, New York. She graduated in 1847 from Troy Female Seminary (now called Russell Sage College). Her family initially was wealthy. Then when her father lost his fortune, she became a teacher.

Slocum married Russell Sage in 1869. He was a financier who was involved in many stock market ventures, railroads, banks, and other businesses. Mr. Sage had begun working in his brother's grocery store when he was 12, after just a few years of schooling. He had saved enough to buy the store in 1837, when he was 21 years old. Later, he became involved in politics, and served four years in the U.S. House of Representatives. In 1857 he left the House to build his fortune. He lived in New York City when they were married.

When Mr. Sage died in 1906, he left his entire estate (then more than $70 million) to Mrs. Sage. She assisted many charities with the fortune. Mrs. Sage was especially interested in the education of women and in church missions. She set up the Russell Sage Foundation in 1907 to find ways to improve social and living conditions in the United States. When the Russell Sage Foundation was established, it held the record as the biggest act of philanthropy ever seen in the U.S.

GA1327

Margaret Slocum Activities

Discussion Questions

Discuss the following questions with your teacher and classmates:

1. What does the word *philanthropy* mean? Look it up in your glossary.

2. Was Mrs. Sage being a responsible citizen when she focused the Foundation on social and living conditions? What about other social problems which may have existed then? Should she have considered them, too?

3. Did she have to give away any of her money?

4. Do you have any obligation as a citizen to give to charities? If you do not, why not? If you do, then why do you? If you have no obligation but do give money to charities, how do you explain your actions?

Imagine and Find Out

List all the charities you can find and tell what they do.

Imagine someone in your family willed a very large amount of money to you. Imagine that you decided to donate some of it to charities. Consider the following:

- What percentage would you donate to charities? What would you do with the rest?
- What charity or charities would you donate to? Why have you selected the ones you have?
- Would you create a new charity and name it after yourself? Why or why not?

Create a new charity and give it a name. Describe below what it does.

GA1327

Gifford Pinchot

One of the United States' early conservationists was Gifford Pinchot (pronounced pin show). Pinchot was born in Connecticut in 1865 and graduated from Yale University in 1889. From Yale, Pinchot went to France to study forestry. When he returned to the U.S., he wasted no time becoming involved in the shaping of public policy toward the nation's wooded areas.

Initially Pinchot worked at the Vanderbilt estate in North Carolina, where he set up one of the country's first forestry programs. Very soon he was appointed to a new National Forest Commission. This Commission was formed to make a plan for the national government's forest reserves. The next year, in 1897, he became chief advisor on forests to the Secretary of the Department of the Interior. From "Interior" he moved to the Department of Agriculture to head the National Forest Service. He stayed there until 1910.

Pinchot used these positions to strengthen the nation's ability to manage its forests and to build a new awareness of conservation problems in the American public. During this time, Pinchot also advised the Philippines on how to manage that country's forests and served on many commissions (including ones which dealt with public land use, the inland waterway system, and the quality of country life). He also helped found the School of Forestry at Yale University. Pinchot became a professor and taught there from 1903 until 1936. He became head of the National Conservation Association in 1910 and remained in that position until 1925.

In 1910 Gifford Pinchot was dismissed as head of the Forest Service by President William H. Taft. He had become embroiled in a controversy which involved the Secretary of the Interior at that time. The Secretary had been charged with conflicts of interest in the decisions he made. Pinchot had been one of those making the charges.

In 1920 Pinchot served as Commissioner of Forestry in Pennsylvania. Then in 1922 Pinchot ran for election and became governor of that state. As governor, Pinchot introduced reforms in government administration and finances. He later served again as governor from 1931 to 1935. Pinchot died in New York City in 1946, at the age of 81.

GA1327

Gifford Pinchot Activities

Discussion Questions

Discuss the following questions with your teacher and classmates:

1. What does the term *public policy* mean? Look in your glossary.

2. What do you suppose motivated Pinchot to work so hard and to accomplish so much?

3. What are *conflicts of interest*? Look in your glossary.

4. What kind of skills are necessary to be an effective manager in government?

5. When someone with a conflict of interest becomes involved in a decision, what should he do?

6. Was Gifford Pinchot a responsible citizen? Why or why not?

Walk, Discover, Take Action

Take a long walk around your neighborhood and community. Take a pencil and paper. Jot down all the environmental problems that you see and those you imagine exist (based on effects that you see). Then brainstorm a list of those actions you can take to do something about the problems. Does anything stop you from doing something about the problems in your neighborhood? Community? School? What can you do about the things that are stopping you? What policy is necessary to help care for our environment?

GA1327

Lucretia Coffin Mott

Lucretia Coffin Mott lived to be 87 years old. She was born in 1793 in Nantucket, Massachusetts. Her father's wish for her was that she "become familiar with the workings of democratic principles." She studied and taught near Poughkeepsie, New York, at a Society of Friends (Quaker) boarding school.

Mott spoke with fervor about such social issues as the abolition of slavery, peace, and the use of alcohol. In 1818 she was accepted as a minister of the Friends. She began to travel across the country to lecture about the causes which concerned her. Then in 1833 Mott helped found the American Anti-Slavery Society and became its president.

Lucretia Mott soon began to meet with opposition. Her views on abolition of slavery led to attempts to revoke her status as a Society of Friends minister. In 1840 she also had trouble making her views known at an Anti-Slavery Convention in London because she was a woman. In 1848, Mott and Elizabeth Cady Stanton helped found the women's rights movement at another antislavery convention held in Seneca Falls, New York.

GA1327

Lucretia Coffin Mott Activities

Discussion Questions

Discuss the following questions with your teacher and classmates:

1. What are *democratic principles*? Look in your glossary.

2. Should Lucretia Mott have stopped fighting to free slaves when she met with opposition? Why do you suppose people opposed what she said?
   - because they felt it was right to enslave people?
   - because she forced them to examine their own beliefs?
   - because they were uncomfortable with changes?

3. How long did you think the women's rights movement had been going on before you read this article? Do you now think that perhaps some other current social issues date back into history much farther than you initially thought? Why might this be so?

What to Say and Not to Say?

How do you decide what to say and what not to say? Do you choose what to say according to whether or not people will like you? Respect you? Agree with you? Want to be your friend? Pay attention to you? Believe you? Remember you? Do you choose what to say and not say because it is right? Good? Just? The truth?

Get a large paper bag, magic markers, and index cards. On the outside of the bag write those things you are willing to say aloud. Do you say it aloud because you know it will get you respect and admiration, or do you say it aloud because you believe in it regardless of what others think of you?

Now think about the things you don't say. On each index card write one of the things you believe in, have an opinion about, or disagree with but don't say aloud because you fear not getting approval or respect, being liked, etc.

How do you feel about keeping many of your opinions and thoughts in a secret bag? How does this affect you? Affect others? Affect communities? If you are willing, then share one or two of your thoughts that you've kept hidden in a "bag" with your teacher and classmates. Does the catastrophe that you imagined happen, or are you pleasantly surprised? Every time you share a thought in your bag with someone else, throw out the index card and write the thought on the outside of your bag.

GA1327

Nicola Sacco and Bartolomeo Vanzetti

Nicola Sacco was born in southern Italy in 1891 and migrated to Massachusetts in 1908 when he was 17. He lived in Milford, Massachusetts, and worked in a shoe factory until 1920, except for one year. In 1917-18, Sacco went to Mexico to avoid the World War I draft.

Bartolomeo Vanzetti was born in northern Italy in 1888. Vanzetti also migrated to the United States in 1908. However, he worked many places before he became a fish peddler in Plymouth, Massachusetts, in 1915. Like Sacco, Vanzetti also went to Mexico to avoid the draft.

Both men became interested in socialism and in working-class movements. Vanzetti was better educated and had been influenced by the writings of Leo Tolstoi, Karl Marx, St. Augustine, Prince Kropotkin, Ernest Renan, etc. He became a philosophical anarchist.

After World War I and the revolutions in Russia, many people in the United States became extremely afraid that the country would also experience a communist revolution. During this period, on April 15, 1920, in Braintree, Massachusetts, two men robbed and killed the paymaster and a guard at a shoe factory and then escaped. The two men were described as "dark, Italian-looking."

Almost three weeks later, on May 5th, Sacco and Vanzetti were arrested and charged with the murders. They had reputations as draft dodgers, radicals, and anarchists. They also fit the descriptions of the criminals. In addition, they were carrying guns when they were arrested.

A year later, on May 31, 1921, their trial began. All the evidence tying the two men to the crime was circumstantial. The testimony of eighteen Italian-born witnesses was ignored by the jury. The trial ended on July 14th. Both men were found guilty of first-degree murder by the jury. The judge sentenced them to death. Sacco and Vanzetti appealed for a new trial, but they were denied one by the same judge. Then in 1925 another convict who had already been sentenced for murder confessed to playing a role in the shoe factory murders.

After Italian-American groups and many other individuals and groups throughout the world protested, the governor of Masachusetts formed an independent committee headed by the president of Harvard University to review the case. In August of 1927 the committee found that the trial had been fair and without prejudice.

As protests grew throughout the United States and around the world, Nicola Sacco and Bartolomeo Vanzetti were electrocuted to death on August 23, 1927.

GA1327

Sacco and Vanzetti Activities

Discussion Questions

Discuss the following questions with your teacher and classmates:

1. What does the phrase *without prejudice* mean?

2. What is *circumstantial evidence*? Look in your glossary.

3. By going to Mexico, did Sacco practice *civil disobedience*?

4. Should personal freedoms in the United States include the freedom to advocate political philosophies which differ from what most people believe? Explain your answer.

5. Should everyone be required to serve in the armed forces when the country is at war? Why or why not?

6. Should you always support the decisions of educated and powerful people? If so, why? If not, why not?

7. Would you feel any differently toward this case if Sacco and Vanzetti were of the same ethnic group as you?

Understanding Differences

With what ethnic group, if any, would you identify yourself? _____

List below all the foods you can think of which we eat with our hands. Next to each food, write *yes* if you are using good table manners when you eat this food with your hands, and *no* if you are not using good manners to eat the food with your hands.

Foods I Eat with My Hands	Good Manners	Bad Manners

Now, think about the ways that people from other ethnic backgrounds, other cultures, other countries, eat these same foods. Do they always eat the foods the same way you do? Do you think that they might think you sometimes have bad manners? Do you think they have bad manners, or do you think they are eating foods the way they have been taught?

_____

_____

_____

_____

GA1327

Write On!

Now list five customs you and your family practice but that not all other families practice. Write a story and include some of these customs as part of the plot. Illustrate your story and read it aloud.

Write an article describing how you see ethnic differences affecting the school which you attend or your town. Write your concerns.

Five Customs My Family and I Practice

1.

2.

3.

4.

5.

 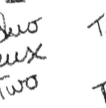 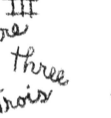  

GA1327

Allan Pinkerton

Allan Pinkerton was born in Scotland in 1819. His father was a police sergeant. He emigrated from Scotland in 1842 to Illinois and then became a cooper. Some time later, while he was working on an uninhabited island, he accidentally discovered a band of counterfeiters. Pinkerton led an effort to capture the counterfeiters, and thus began his career as a detective.

Interestingly, Pinkerton was an opponent of slavery. When he began to work in law enforcement in 1846, he turned his cooper's shop into a "way station" for the Underground Railroad. In this way he helped slaves to become free men.

He became the first detective ever on the Chicago police force in 1850. When a wave of railroad robberies occurred, Pinkerton set up his own business, the Pinkerton National Detective Agency. At that time Pinkerton was a pioneer in a new kind of business in the United States. His agency solved many railroad crimes, and in 1861 he even uncovered a plot to assassinate Abraham Lincoln as he passed through Baltimore on his way to be inaugurated President.

As the Civil War started, General George McClellan tapped Pinkerton to organize a secret service and head a department of counterespionage in the government. In 1862 Pinkerton left government to return to managing his business. He investigated many cases of fraud and claims against the government.

After the war, Pinkerton's agency began to specialize. The agency became well-known for its work against labor movements and labor unions. The agency was often used by employers for strikebreaking. The agency was primarily responsible for crushing the Molly Maguires labor rights movement in the Pennsylvania anthracite coalfields. Pinkerton's books were *The Molly Maguires and the Detectives* written in 1877 and *Strikers, Communists, Tramps and Detectives* in 1878. Allan Pinkerton died in Chicago in 1884.

Allan Pinkerton Activities

Discussion Questions

Discuss the following questions with your teacher and classmates:

1. What is a *cooper*? Look in your glossary.

2. Why is counterfeiting illegal?

3. Was it Pinkerton's duty as a citizen to assist General McClellan? Why or why not?

4. Was Pinkerton a responsible citizen when he left his business for government service?

5. Are there any circumstances when it is acceptable for a government to spy on its own people? If so, describe them. Draw a picture to show the situation.

6. Try to imagine why the coalfield workers might have attempted to organize unions. Try to imagine the reasons the owners of coal mines might have had for wishing to prevent the workers from organizing. Now try to imagine how politicians might have viewed the Molly Maguires situation.

7. What is *counterespionage*? *Labor union*? *Strikebreaking*? Look in your glossary.

Be Your Own Detective

Use your library to find out what the Underground Railroad was. Share your findings with your teacher and class. Were the people involved in running the Underground Railroad practicing civil disobedience?

Write a script to role-play with your classmates. Use one of the themes below.

- A group of people on the Underground Railroad are in big danger.
- A member of a secret service discovers something very important.
- You are part of an espionage ring helping your government.
- You are attempting to organize a labor strike but fear that paid informants are working where you do.

GA1327

Delia Bacon

Delia Bacon was born in Ohio in 1811. She moved to Connecticut as a girl and attended Catherine E. Beecher's school for girls. Bacon wanted to establish her own school. She tried several times but failed in each attempt. Eventually she became a writer and a lecturer on history and literature.

Bacon gradually developed a theory that Shakespeare's works actually had been written by a group of well-known public figures led by a man named Francis Bacon. The group, which included Sir Walter Raleigh and Edmund Spenser, attributed their work to an "obscure" actor named William Shakespeare "largely for political reasons."

With some encouragement from Ralph Waldo Emerson, Delia Bacon became convinced that her theory was true. In 1853 she went to England to prove it. She lived there in poverty for three years while she investigated. Then in 1856, on the verge of completing her plan to open Shakespeare's grave—to look for documents which would prove her theory correct, she said—she suddenly abandoned her plan without explanation.

Another American writer, Nathaniel Hawthorne, who in 1856 was the American government's representative in Liverpool, England, "took pity on her, lent her money, and arranged for publication of her book *The Philosophy of the Plays of Shakespeare Unfolded*." As soon as the book appeared, Bacon went insane, never learning that the book was widely ridiculed when it was published. She was taken home to Ohio in 1858, where she died the next year. The idea which had obsessed her throughout her later life eventually took on a life of its own, gaining new believers as time passed.

Delia Bacon Activities

Discussion Questions

Discuss the following questions with your teacher and classmates:

1. What did Delia Bacon contribute to her community? Was she a responsible citizen? Was she a burden in any way?

2. What do you think led her to pursue her theory?

3. What role might her earlier failure to establish a school have played in her persistence in her theory?

4. What did she have in common with Francis Bacon?

Success and Failure

Write your definitions of *success* and *failure*. Compare these with your classmates'. See if some of the ways in which you perceive your failures are really successes. Ask yourself where your ideas of success and failure come from?

For example: I'm not the person with the best grades in my class, but I work hard and study diligently and do the best I can.

Success   **Failure**

GA1327

Glossary

censorship	to prohibit what is considered morally or otherwise objectionable
circumstantial evidence	evidence not bearing directly on the fact in dispute but on other circumstances which the judge or jury might infer
citizen	a native or naturalized person of a city or town, especially one entitled to its privileges; native or naturalized person who gives allegiance to a government and is entitled to protection from it.
citizenship	the status of being a citizen and having the rights, privileges, and duties of a citizen
civic	of or relating to a citizen, a city, citizenship, or civil affairs
civil	of or relating to citizens
civilian	one not on active duty in a military, police, or fire fighting force
civilize	to acquire the customs and activities of a civil community
civil defense	plans or activities organized by civilians for the protection of population and property in times of such emergencies as war, floods, etc.
civil disobedience	the refusal to obey certain governmental laws or demands for the purpose of influencing legislation or government policy, characterized by such nonviolent techniques as boycotting, picketing, and nonpayment of taxes
civil liberty	the liberty of an individual to exercise those rights guaranteed by the laws of a country
civil rights	the nonpolitical rights of a citizen especially the rights of personal liberty guaranteed to U.S. citizens by the 13th and 14th amendments to the Constitution and by acts of Congress
civil service	the administrative service of a government or international agency exclusive of the armed forces
civil war	a war between opposing groups of citizens of the same country or nation
conflict of interest	a clash or controversy between interests of people
counterespionage	spying undertaken to detect and act against enemy spying
cooper	one who makes wooden barrels
Darwin's theory of natural selection	Charles Darwin's theory stating that species of plants and animals having characteristics advantageous for survival in a specific environment make up an increasing proportion of their species in that environment

GA1327

democratic principles	certain truths or laws promoting the interests of the people
disobedience	the fact of not obeying
labor strike	a stopping of work by employees, in support of demands made upon their employer
labor union	organization of people who earn wages formed for the purpose of serving their class interests with wages and working conditions in mind
militia	a citizen army
naturalized citizen	person who originally had citizenship of one country who then attains citizenship of another country
philanthropy	love of mankind; the effort to increase the well-being of mankind as with charitable aid and/or donations
public policy	government objectives and priorities which are reflected in what the government does and the laws it makes
strikebreaking	providing an employer with workers to break up a strike
vigilante	a member of an informal council exercising police power for the capture, trial, and punishment of criminal offenders

GA1327

Bibliography

Aline Brothier Morris Fund. *American Citizenship*. New Haven, CT: Yale University Press, 1933, 70 pp.

Bellah, Robert N., et. al. *Habits of the Heart*. New York: Harper & Row, 1985, 355 pp.

de Kay, James T. *Meet Martin Luther King, Jr.* New York: Random House, 1969, 89 pp.

Brogan, D.W. *Citizenship Today: England, France, the United States*. Chapel Hill, NC: The University of North Carolina Press, 1960, 116 pp.

The First Church of Christ, Scientist, *The Christian Science Monitor*. Boston, MA: The Christian Science Publishing Society, various issues.

The International Thesaurus of Quotations compiled by Rhoda Thomas Tripp. New York: Thomas Y. Crowell Company, 1970.

Halberstam, David. *The Best and the Brightest*. New York: Penguin Books, 1972, 831 pp.

Mitchell, Arnold. *The Nine American Lifestyles*. New York: Warner Books, 1983, 302 pp.

New York City Board of Education, Division of Curriculum and Instruction. *Citizenship in New York City*. Brooklyn, NY: Board of Education of the City of New York, 1982, 306 pp.

_____. *Scholastic Update*. New York: Scholastic, Inc., various issues.

Taft, William Howard. *Four Aspects of Civic Duty*. New Haven, CT: Yale University Press, 1906, 111 pp.

Van Doren, Charles, editor. *Webster's American Biographies*. Springfield, MA: G. & C. Merriam Company, 1979, 1233 pp.

_____. *The Wall Street Journal*. New York: Dow Jones & Company, Inc., July 3, 1990.

GA1327